To Quinton,

Thank you for your support.
Thank you for thinking BIG.
Much Success!

Farrell J. White
8/23/11

Advance Praise for As BIG As It Gets

"Today on my long trip back from the east coast, I finished reading your manuscript. First, let me say, wow! What a legacy! Your leadership of BIG was transforming. The passion you have for the organization is apparent, and we all know that you can't have that kind of success without passion for the organization and the people. What I really appreciated was how you skillfully demonstrated the many qualities of a successful leader. You talked about commitment, the investment of time, time away from family, skilled administrative assistants, and the ability to be a pro at networking. I really enjoyed reading it. As I had shared with you, I did not know a lot about BIG. After reading your manuscript, I thought, I really missed out!"
- Loretta Martin, former Chief, United States Probation Department, Los Angeles

"As BIG As It Gets" is an empowerment tool for growing future leaders. A legacy of lessons learned and leadership experiences from a results driven leader – the "One and Only" Farrell Chiles. Documenting your journey and tenure as Chairman of the Board of Directors for five terms will surely set a standard for others to emulate. You set precedence with your service and now with your pen ship. Thanks for the gift of "selfless-service" and volunteerism that is truly "As BIG As It Gets!"
- Amicitia Maloon-Gibson, President, ATIC & MG Center for Excellence

"I believe you hit the "Nail on the Head" with your book. I, being a member of the Board of Directors, can say without a doubt that you were a leader amongst leaders and handled that responsibility very well. I now realize that even with the short time that I spent as the board chair – I needed your support and guidance to manage so many

different personalities. I want to thank you again for your mentorship and friendship."
- Gary Blackmon, Department of Defense, BIG Chairman of the Board (2008)

"The excerpts are very interesting. Your recount of BIG activities in 2005 evoked some emotion: I remember being impressed with your continued successes when you were re-elected in 2005. I can't wait to read the rest of the book. I believe "As BIG As It Gets" will be the closest many of us will get to such a powerful experience in Blacks In Government. Thanks for giving me a preliminary view of your story."
- Cynthia Davis, BIG National Secretary (2003-2007)

"This is as "BIG As It Gets" in Blacks In Government, I felt as though you took me on a voyage in this book. Mr. Chiles, you captured the essence of what it is like to be on top of your game. It's like a chess game, the ultimate aim in the game is to win by analyzing and overpowering your opponent; and you master that technique. Your book is going to be a "BIG" hit on the book tour."
- Martha Ervin, Department of the Army

"Yes. This will be good reading for sure. Chapter 8 brought back so many memories! I found myself smiling while reading the Board Chair nominees' responses to the various questions asked of them and the vote count that followed. I vividly remember your demeanor (poised and confident) and how you effortlessly answered the questions. Thank you for sharing, Farrell."
- Nancy Tillman, Federal Deposit Insurance Corporation

"As BIG As It Gets" illustrates passion in leadership and the powerful effects of paradigm shifts. Mr. Chiles has written a very readable book that contains a rich assortment of introspective personal assessments

and mature reflections based on practical experiences as a leader. The contents of this book will serve to inspire and motivate emerging organizational leaders for years to come."
- Ida Tyree-Hyche, Department of the Army

As BIG As It Gets

A Chairman of the Board's Rise and Tenure at the Top – Lessons in Leadership

Farrell J. Chiles

Hardcover ISBN: 978-1-60910-445-0
Paperback ISBN: 978-1-60910-265-4

Printed in the United States of America.

BookLocker.com, Inc.
2011

DEDICATION

I dedicate this book…

To my father, James H. Chiles (1928-2007), my role model
To my mother, Louise Chiles (a mother's love)
To my wife, Verdene Chiles (always there for me)
To my daughter, Tracy Chiles McGhee (the joy of my life)
To my granddaughter, Sasha Ariel Alston (my best friend in the whole wide world)
To my brother and sisters (always have my back)

ACKNOWLEDGMENTS

To the National Board of Director members with whom I have served, who helped me grow while in the position and who continuously supported me for five consecutive terms.

To J B. Larkins - my mentor. Thank you for seeing potential in me and opening your doors to me. To Maude Larkins – thank you for the grits and pound cakes.

I am deeply grateful to three wonderful women who assisted me during my tenure. To Ms. Kimberly Best-Tuten (the starter, 2002); Ms. Rebecca Lewis McDonald (the connector, 2003-2004); and Ms. Barbara Johnson Cox (the closer, 2005-2006). Each served as my Executive Assistant and brought professionalism, dedication, and commitment to the position that aided me to fulfill my leadership role efficiently.

To my fellow Army Warrant Officers who responded to my call and became my support base in Blacks In Government – Roxana Beattie, Raymond Benson, Mary Carter, Martha Ervin, Rowmell Hughes, Belynda Lindsey, Lynda Thompson, and Ida Tyree-Hyche. All became Life Members in BIG.

To Dawn Lawson and Cynthia Davis, National Secretaries during my tenure as Chair. Working with them made my job enjoyable and easier. Both are outstanding professionals.

To Thomas Walton, who served as my Board parliamentarian and as an advisor to me during my years as the Chairman. Sir, your advice and counsel helped me through the difficult times.

To J. David Reeves. When we were elected Chair and Vice Chair in 2002, we were labeled the “dynamic duo”. We served on the board together for six years. Your support was greatly appreciated.

Finally, to my BIG family: I am forever indebted to you for accepting me when I was essentially a stranger and accompanying me on this magnificent journey.

Thank you.

Farrell J. Chiles

Contents

INTRODUCTION

This book is not an autobiography. It is not a memoir. Nor is it a history book. It's about my tenure as the Board Chair of the National Organization of Blacks In Government and the years leading up to my election as Chair. Although this book does not purport to be an official record, excerpts from Board meeting transcripts are used to highlight certain events that occurred during my tenure. The book chronicles my experiences and events during BIG's emergence as the leading organization for public service employees.

PART ONE

Chapter 1: The Election 2002

"Leaders don't wait. They shape their own frontiers. The bigger the challenge, the greater the opportunity." - Anonymous

Blacks In Government
National Board of Directors Meeting
Embassy Suites Hotel
Kansas City, Missouri
Friday, January 11, 2002

Excerpts from the official transcript:

Ms. Ellen Dyson: Good morning. The meeting is officially called to order at 9:20 a.m., Friday, January 11, 2002. From the agenda, we're going to ask Mr. Thomas Walton to give us our opening prayer…

Ms. Ellen Dyson: The next item on the agenda is the election of the Board Chair and Vice Chair. And now I relinquish my seat as the 2001 Board Chair and turn it over to Mr. Thomas Walton for the election.

Mr. Thomas Walton: Thank you, Madam Chair. We are about to receive nominations for the Chair of the Board of Directors. In accordance with our National Constitution, Section 1 of that article [Article VI], it states, "The Chair of the Board serves as the Chair of the Board of Directors, officially transmits the policies which have been approved by the Board of Directors, recommends to the Board of Directors changes in policies and procedures, presents the organization's annual report to the annual Delegates Assembly, appoints committee chairs of the Board with the consent of the Board, and is an ex-officio member of the board committees.

Requires reports on the activities of the Regional Councils and the chapters through the Board of Directors from the regions and board committees; performs such functions and exercises such other activities as may be prescribed by the Board of Directors. The Chair of the board cannot be a member of the Executive Committee."

The floor is now open for nominations for the office of Chair of the National Board of Directors. I recognize Mr. Oscar Williams.

Mr. Oscar Williams: Oscar Williams, Region V, I nominate Ellen G. Dyson from Region V.

Mr. Thomas Walton: Ellen G. Dyson is nominated. Mr. Larkins.

Mr. J.B. Larkins: J.B. Larkins, Region IX. I recommend Farrell Chiles.

Mr. Thomas Walton: Mr. Farrell Chiles has been nominated. Ms. Hampton.

Ms. David Hampton: David Hampton, Greater Kansas City Chapter. I nominate Julius Crouch.

Mr. Thomas Walton: Mr. Julius Crouch has been nominated. Any further nominations?

Mr. Thomas Walton: On second call, for the office of the Chair of the Board of Directors?

Mr. Thomas Walton: Third and final call?

(No response)

Mr. Thomas Walton: Seeing no hands and no one is speaking, we declare the nominations to be closed for the office of Chair of the National Board of Directors on the names of Ms. Ellen G. Dyson, Mr. Farrell Chiles, and Mr. Julius Crouch.

The policy requires that it be done by secret ballot. We're going to ask now if Ms. Dorris and Mr. Davis will pass the ballots to the Board members only.

Mr. Thomas Walton: According to – we have 23 present. We have two with excused absence. That means there should be 23 votes, or the voting cannot exceed 23. And we need 12.

Mr. Abe Joseph: Question. Being new to the Board, do the candidates get up and give a presentation?

Mr. Thomas Walton: We can if that's your pleasure, sir. They can still pass out the ballots.

Mr. Abe Joseph: Two minutes.

Mr. Thomas Walton: By consent of the Board, is that all right? Two minutes for each candidate all right?

(Members responded in the affirmative)

Mr. Thomas Walton: At this time, we will hear from candidate Ellen G. Dyson.

Ms. Ellen Dyson: Well, I noticed everybody—I have everybody else's (referring to campaign flyers). I didn't do one. My theory was, if you don't know me by now, you'll never know me. I almost brought my record by Harold Melvin and the Blue Notes.

I am seeking another term as the Chair of the Board so I can continue with some of the organizational structure that I think—I would like to think that I have brought to the Board. That was my purpose.

I don't make any promises about what I am going to do as Board Chair, the programs that I'm going to implement, because according with the constitution and my way of thinking, that is not my job.

My job is to serve as your leader, to communicate your ideas. And I took it further than just chairing a meeting. I also felt it was my responsibility, in addition to communicating the ideas, was to keep us on track in between meetings, as well as make sure – do the things in advance to make sure that our meetings were set up correctly and that they ran smoothly.

And if I'm re-elected, I will continue to communicate the decisions of the Board, to report to those who require – that we're required to report to the actions that we took on the Board, to continue to defend the actions of the Board to the Executive Committee and the delegates to the best of my ability. It will be business as usual if I'm re-elected. Thank you.

Mr. Thomas Walton: Mr. Farrell Chiles.

Mr. Farrell Chiles: Good morning. I seek your vote as the Chair of the Board for this upcoming year. I represent change. I represent new leadership, new opportunities, new growth for the organization, new energy.

I know what the roles and responsibilities of a Chair are. I've studied over the last year the organization, the personalities, the business, the culture. I've taken notes. I've talked to people. I've listened and I've learned.

Leadership is not new to me. I've been a leader in other organizations. I'm a leader in this organization. I believe I can bring to the Board and to the National organization of BIG the kind of professionalism and the kind of leadership that we need as we continue to grow and become that world class organization that we talk about.

So, in essence, what I'm saying, vote for me because new leadership is required as we go forward; and in doing so, we make a statement, not only to ourselves but to the National organization and its members that we are for moving forward and that we do accept new people into the organization and provide opportunities for them to grow as BIG grows. Thank you.

Mr. Thomas Walton: Mr. Julius Crouch.

Mr. Julius Crouch: Good morning. I sent each of you an e-mail. I've handed out to each of you this morning a flier stating where I stand.

You noticed I didn't say I. You noticed I said we. And I think it's time that we, as a Board, who are responsible for the management of Blacks In Government to get back to basics.

Following 9-11 nothing is ever going to be the same again. Let's forget about that.

BIG has a job to do. BIG started doing this job back in 1975 and it's fixing to get hot in the kitchen again.

We need to focus on our goals and objectives. One of the things we used to do on the Board was before we approved any budget item, we made sure that it was addressing a goal and an objective; and we need to start making sure that's happening again. Why? Because I guarantee you, the IRS is going to be looking a little bit closer at us. And as long as we're supporting our goals and objectives and properly doing the things we need to do, we can ensure that we are getting the job done.

We are a member service organization. If the Board does not take the leadership in seeing that services are provided to our membership, then who will? We need to ensure that we provide more services to the individual members.

BIG has focused over the years on civil rights issues. We have to fight discrimination. That whole process is changing. If we don't start putting some things in place today, we're in trouble and our members are in trouble.

The Board does not implement programs, but a lot of the programs that are now in place started at the Board of Directors, were developed at the Board, given to the Executive Committee to implement.

We can be a program for career development and to address civil rights issues, and we need to be doing that because that is why we were founded.

I'm not only asking for your vote, but if elected, I'm asking you to work harder than you've ever worked before to carry this organization to the next level. Thank you.

Mr. Thomas Walton: Thank you to all three candidates…Ladies and gentlemen, the ballots that you have in front of you, you may only vote for one candidate. Please follow the instructions that are there. Please print clearly and vote for only one.

The ballots will be collected by Ms. Dorris and Mr. Davis.

Mr. Thomas Walton: Are there anymore ballots? Anyone that has not finished their ballot yet?

(No response)

Mr. Thomas Walton: Thank you. Ms. Mc Duffy and Mr. Wilson, would you please observe the counting of the ballots?

Are you ready Mr. Davis, Ms. Dorris? We will count them out loud and then you will hand them to either Ms. Mc Duffy or Mr. Wilson.

Ms. Mamie Dorris: Call them as we do them?

Mr. Thomas Walton: Yes.

Mr. Melvin Davis: Vote for Mr. Chiles.

Ms. Dyson.

Chiles.

Dyson.

Chiles.

Dyson.

Dyson.

Crouch.

Crouch.

Chiles.
Chiles.
Chiles.
Chiles.
Chiles.
Crouch.
Dyson.
Dyson.
Crouch.
Chiles.
Dyson.
Chiles.
Chiles.
Chiles.

Total of 23 votes: 7 for Ms. Dyson; 12 cast for Chiles; and 4 votes cast for Crouch.

Mr. Thomas Walton: It was required that there be at least 12 votes for a majority since we had 23 voting. Then I declare that Mr. Chiles has been elected as Chair of the National Board of Directors.

(Applause)

After I was duly elected to serve as Chair, it was time to elect the Vice Chair of the National Board of Directors. The Vice Chair of the Board assumes and performs all the duties and functions of the Chair in the event of the Chair's absence or disability. Mr. J. David Reeves, Mr. Danny Thomas, and Mr. Ralph Browne were nominated.

With 15 votes, J. David Reeves was elected as Vice-Chair. Together we took our oath:

"I"

Mr. Farrell Chiles: Farrell Chiles

Mr. J. David Reeves: J. David Reeves

Mr. Thomas Walton: Do solemnly affirm that I will adhere to the mandates of the National Constitution of Blacks In Government, the District of Columbia Code and all bylaws. I also affirm that I will carry out the duties of the office of Board Chair –

Mr. J. David Reeves: Board Vice Chair.

Mr. Thomas Walton: (Continuing) – or any other outlined duties that are implied in the official document previously stated. I will do this to the best of my knowledge, skills, and ability. I further affirm that at the end of my term and/or resignation or removal or election or installation of any successor in office that I will immediately turn over to my successor all books, papers, monies, and documents or any other properties of Blacks In Government in my possession or under my control. All these things I do solemnly affirm.

(Members responded)

Mr. Thomas Walton: To the members of the National Board of Directors, I present to you your Chair and Vice Chair for the Year 2002, Mr. Chiles, Mr. J. David Reeves.

(Applause)

* *

I was the newly elected Chairman of the National Board of Directors of Blacks In Government. It was time to get to work.

Chapter 2: The Beginning 1998 - 1999

"Leadership is not about imposing authority. It's about building relationships, where people are inspired, encouraged, and influenced to follow." – Dr. Perry W. Thomas, Sc.D

I first heard of BIG in July 1993. I was employed with the Veterans Administration Medical Center (VAMC) in West Los Angeles as a management analyst. One of my co-workers was Priscilla Martin, a transplant from St. Louis. Priscilla was a former Missouri state employee who had spent time in Washington, D.C. on a special project and was familiar with BIG and at one time belonged to the local St. Louis chapter. She mentioned that the National Training Conference would be in Los Angeles the next month in August. So, I contacted the National Office for information which was faxed to me. I then contacted the VAMC's training department about the availability of funding to attend the conference. The answer was there weren't any funds available. However, that did not deter me from attending the conference. I just went and hung out in the lobby, in the exhibit area, and in the Bonaventure Hotel bar. I met wonderful people from all over the country and from different governmental agencies representing a wide variety of governmental occupations and grades. I got to network, have some interesting conversations, exchange information, and enjoy myself. And, there was no cost to me or my agency.

Later, in 1998, I was employed with the Department of Army when a former co-worker of mine, Patricia Ferguson from the VAMC, called and asked me to join a newly formed chapter of BIG - The West Los Angeles VAMC Chapter. She forwarded me an application. Upon reviewing the application, instead of taking out a regular membership, I decided to take out a Life Membership. The cost was $250.00. In comparison to other organizations in which I held Life Memberships, this was a great deal. So I mailed my application to the National Office and with an effective date of March 12, 1998, I had joined and became a Life Member of Blacks In Government.

I worked in Los Alamitos, CA and the chapter was in West Los Angeles, approximately 40 miles away. The chapter held its meetings monthly during lunchtimes. Most of the members were employed by the VA and communicated regularly with each other via the VA's internal e-mail system. Quite frankly, I was out of the loop, which made it difficult to participate in chapter activities.

My agency provided funding for me to attend the 1998 National Training Conference in Washington, D.C. The conference was held at the Washington Hilton hotel located on Connecticut Avenue, NW. I was notified that I would be receiving my Life Membership Plaque at the Opening Plenary Session on that Monday morning. We were seated by regions and chapters in a designated area. I sat next to Joseph Latham, the West Los Angeles VAMC Chapter president. We were the first two members in the chapter to become Life Members. I remember feeling proud walking across the stage to accept my plaque. Afterwards, there were group photos; however, I did not participate in them. Later, I received phone calls from friends who saw me on C-SPAN accepting my plaque. Overall, I really enjoyed the conference. Once again, I met some outstanding people and the networking was excellent.

As far as active participation, Blacks In Government was not one of my priority organizations in 1998. I belonged to the United States Army Warrant Officers Association (USAWOA) and the Reserve Officers Association (ROA) among other organizations. I was a member of the United States Army Reserve. As a matter of fact, I was employed as a military technician at the 63d Regional Readiness Command. It is a civilian, dual status, military technician position, and as a requirement of employment, I had to belong to an Army Reserve unit. Since 1990, I had given a lot of focus to my military career and dual status civilian career. In October 1998, I was awarded the United States Army Warrant Officers Association's CW4 Albert M. Holcombe Memorial Award as the Warrant Officer of the Year. I was the first African-American male to receive the award. In 1994, Mary Carter became the first African American to receive the honor. Mary and I were founding members of the USAWOA Southern California Chapter in 1993. She became the chapter's first president and went on to serve on the USAWOA Board of Directors from 1994-1997.

In January 1999, I was awarded the Reserve Officers Association's (ROA) Warrant Officer of the Year honor at a luncheon during its annual Mid-Winter Conference at the Washington D.C. Hilton. I was very pleased that my daughter and granddaughter were able to attend a reception. I had the distinction of being the first recipient of the award and the competition was very stiff.

Sometime during the April timeframe, I faxed a press release announcing that I was the winner of the award to the National Office. The next month, I was on temporary duty (TDY) attending a two-week personnel course at Fort McCoy, Wisconsin. On a daily basis, I would check my phone messages back at the office and one day I had a message from a Dawn Lawson, who I did not know at the time. I promptly returned the call and Ms. Lawson informed me that the National President has asked her to follow-up with me for a story on my achievement. Ms. Lawson was a member of the National Communications Committee. I was impressed. Dawn interviewed me over the phone and asked me to provide her with a photo and I responded that I would as soon as I returned to California, which I did.

For the 1999 National Training Conference, my agency sponsored three people. I, one other person from Southern California and another from Northern California were selected. The conference was held at the New Orleans Hilton Riverside Hotel. I was still out of the loop as a chapter member and was not a delegate to the Delegates Assembly. As a matter of fact, I did not know about the Delegates Assembly or about any of the organization's politics. I didn't know any National officers and barely the names of the regional representatives. Nevertheless, I networked and began getting to know other BIG members from around the country.

I remember not being able to attend the closing plenary session in the main banquet room and had to sit in the overflow room. The closing plenary session keynote speaker was TV personality and Author Tavis Smiley and he came to the overflow room prior to going to the main room to welcome us and say a few remarks. At the conference, the 1999 summer issue of the BIG Reporter was distributed and, low and behold, an article about me appeared in the magazine. The article was not 100% accurate. I was not afforded the opportunity to review it before publication. But it was a good article. I had received national exposure.

Overall, I was impressed with the number of attendees at the conference and their professionalism. Yet after the conference, I went back to California and BIG still was not put on my priority list of organizations.

Patricia Ferguson, my former co-worker at the VA, called and invited me to attend a Region IX Council Meeting in San Diego scheduled for October 1999. The meeting would start on Friday evening with EEO (Equal Employment Opportunity) training and the business meeting would start on Saturday morning. I attended the Friday evening training and upon completion, went to my room. From what I heard, several people went to dinner together and the topic of the next day's regional elections came up. People at the dinner were looking for someone to run against the incumbent. Patricia Ferguson suggested me. She knew that I had leadership and people skills and she thought I would make an excellent regional council president. She convinced others at the dinner to ask me to run for the position.

During the first break at the meeting the next day, Donna Thomason, one of the Regional Directors, approached me and gave me the background on the previous evening's dinner discussion and asked me to consider running for Regional Council President. I was not a chapter officer. I was not a regional council representative. I had never read any by-laws. My attendance at the meeting was a response to the request of a former co-worker. I told Ms. Thomason that I didn't believe that I could win. But, if she could gather the votes, then I would accept the nomination. We went back into the meeting and the elections were the next order of business. There was no time to shake hands or sell my candidacy one-on-one. The incumbent president was nominated; the Vice-President was nominated, and I was nominated by the President of my chapter. Each candidate had five minutes to make a presentation. This was the first time that many of the attendees had heard me speak and most knew very little about me. I introduced myself, gave a verbal resume of my past experiences in leadership positions in other organizations, and asked the representatives to vote for me. I didn't believe that I could win and I didn't. The incumbent was re-elected with 19 votes, I gathered 15 votes, and the Vice-President received 1 vote. I would have won with three more votes. But those three votes were miles away. I went home that Saturday evening and BIG went to the bottom of my priority list of organizations (again).

Then, J.B Larkins entered the picture. J.B. Larkins was at the regional council meeting and was impressed with my presentation. J.B. was serving on the National Board of Directors and was the founder and first president of the Los Angeles/Long Beach Area Chapter. The chapter was once the largest chapter in BIG with a membership of over 360. That number had dwindled down to eight members. The membership was comprised mostly of the employees at the Long Beach Navy Shipyard. Due to the Department of Defense's BRAC (Base Realignment and Closure) the shipyard closed and the employees either retired, transferred to other local agencies, accepted positions in other parts of the country, or moved on to other careers (staying in the local area). The chapter had gone south and with only eight members, it was on the verge of losing its charter. J.B. called me at work and asked me to join the chapter and to become its president. He promised me that I would have the support of the chapter membership. I told him that I was willing to consider his proposal and he invited me to have a breakfast meeting at his house on a Saturday in November. I asked him was he would be serving grits. He said yes and I accepted his invitation.

Six or seven people were at that Saturday morning meeting and J.B. introduced me to those in attendance and then recommended me for chapter president. There were no objections. I was elected unanimously. Everyone appeared to be happy with my decision to take on the leadership role. Perhaps that was the case since they all had the opportunity to assume a leadership role well before I came on the scene, and had not.

My first order of business was to get some of the people in my circle to join the chapter. So, I made phone calls and sent e-mails and within two weeks, the membership had increased to fourteen. The next meeting in December was again a Saturday morning breakfast over J.

B. Larkins' home (with grits on the menu). I was sworn in as chapter president and my term began in January 2000.

Chapter 3: Chapter President 2000

"Contrary to the opinion of many people, leaders are not born. Leaders are made, and they are made by effort and hard work." – Vince Lombardi

On January 1, 2000, I began my term as the president of the Los Angeles/Long Beach Area Chapter of Blacks In Government. By my first meeting, the membership had grown from eight members in November 1999 to fourteen members in January 2000. However, I knew that several other people that I had recruited had sent their application and transfers to the National Office and the membership would reach 24 by the time the transactions were processed.

At the January 2000 chapter meeting, we decided that we would have an all-day planning meeting in March to determine what would be our goals for the year 2000 and to come up with an action plan to achieve our objectives. One of the members, Sheila Medina, volunteered to have the meeting at her house in Ladera Heights, an upscale community in Los Angeles.

I was at a meeting (I forget which one) and overheard someone mention that their organization had received a grant from the Census Bureau. I inquired about the procedures for a grant and submitted a proposal. The chapter received a $2,500 grant from the Los Angeles Regional Support Census 2000 Center. The grant enabled the chapter to purchase 2,450 coffee mugs with the "Census 2000" and "BIG" logo and the motto "Count On Me" inscribed on each mug. We designated March 26, 2000 as "Census Sunday" and distributed the mugs to several African-American churches in the Los Angeles/Long Beach area to include the Crenshaw Christian Center pastored by Rev. Frederick K.C. Price. We received good exposure and a write-up in the Spring 2000 issue of the BIG Reporter.

By February, we had established a Federal Recognition Agency Program and met with the twelve largest Federal agency heads in the

Los Angeles area to present our 10- Point Plan. We also became a listed affiliate organization of the Greater Los Angeles Federal Executive Board.

In March, on a Saturday morning, we met at Sheila Medina's home as planned. Sheila had a mobile catering company cater breakfast (including grits). The breakfast was delicious. We met by her pool with flip charts ready to do the business of Blacks In Government. The meeting lasted from 8:00 am to 3:00 pm. There were about 20 people in attendance. The chapter was growing. We also had lunch and it was delicious too. We left the meeting focused and energized. We set a goal of 125 members by the end of the year and I appointed Shirley Lamb from the Los Angeles Air Force Base to serve as the Membership Chair. Our other goals were:

- gain 25 Life Members
- get 12 members to attend the 2000 National Training Conference
- participate in at least one national program
- achieve full delegation to Regional meetings (three voting members)
- participate in leadership roles in the 2001 NTC in Los Angeles
- conduct at least on training seminar on a topic of membership interest.

My major focus was to market the organization to the public sector community and create an agenda to provide the broadest exposure of the chapter. In April, I started a quarterly newsletter called "BIG Connections". The newsletter was my "propaganda" piece. I got a local printing company to do the layout and printing as an "In Kind" donation for the first year, with a promise to get later funding to pay for future publications. My "creditability" was on the line, so to speak. The newsletter consisted on 16 pages with articles contributed by chapter members and my contacts and network within and outside of BIG. Each printing produced 300 copies which were distributed to chapter members, Region IX chapter presidents, local federal agency heads, prospective members, the National Board of Director members, the

National Executive Committee members, and to other influential and key communicators that I could think of to send a copy. The newsletter was supposed to put the Los Angeles/Long Beach Area Chapter on the map and, it did. It was a classy newsletter, very professionally done. The first issue of the BIG Connections hit the press in April 2000.

In May, we presented our first Public Service Recognition Awards (PSRA) to four individuals (three chapter members) for their excellence in public service and to one federal agency (U.S. Customs – Long Beach) for its program in fostering a positive image of government service. The intent of the PSRA was to provide recognition to our members who seldom received awards or recognition at their agencies. We presented each award at the recipients' agency in front of their peers and bosses. The agency award was given to the agency to get more buy-in to BIG and get unspoken commitment to support our programs to include sending its employees to the National Training Conference. We were on a roll! We partnered with four other professional organizations and hosted quarterly financial workshops conducted by Charles Schwab, Inc. to our memberships and the community. The workshops were well-attended and Schwab fed the attendees well. On Memorial Day, the chapter honored the family of Captain David K. Carlisle, an African-American West Point graduate and Korean War Veteran, by laying a wreath at his grave site in a ceremony at the Los Angeles National Cemetery. We were making news and our membership was increasing. By June 15th, we had 105 members.

Region IX held its quarterly (July) Council meeting in Sacramento, CA. Donna Thomason, a Region IX Director, was not at the meeting. One of the new chapter presidents began to complain about the lack of responsiveness that he had received from Ms. Thomason. Others jumped on the complaint bandwagon. I *thought* that I saw an opportunity. Mentally, I began counting the chapters that were part of this complaint session. After returning home from the meeting, I sent e-mails to every chapter president (except Ms. Thomason) advising them that I was running for the National Board of Directors. I received some positive feedback, but I wanted to hear from Toni Martin, the president of the Sacramento Metro Chapter. Her chapter was historically the largest chapter in the region, usually with over one hundred members. I needed her support. I called Toni and she informed me that she was considering running for the position. I didn't believe that I could win without her support and chapter votes. She was also very influential with other chapters that she had assisted and supported in their development. I was persistent. I also knew that most people in the region did not contest incumbents. I had done so in the previous October and lost. On the other hand, I did not have a base then, but now I did. I was a chapter president (previously the smallest chapter, less than a year ago) and now the largest chapter in the region with sixteen delegate votes. With Toni's eight to sixteen votes, I was unstoppable. I continued to press Toni and she finally agreed to support me and I believed her. Through my analysis, my magic number was twenty. Based on the region's authorized delegates, the history of actual votes, I had to ensure that my chapter had a full complement of sixteen votes (delegates). The most employees that my agency ever sent were three. I requested nine. Luckily, my commander, a two-star Army Reserve general, was a civilian GS-15 at Fort Huachuca, Arizona and was familiar with Blacks In Government and our National Training Conference. He had sent his employees to the NTC and BIG had received high marks from the attendees. He approved the request for nine people to go. Every agency member who was a Life Member and wanted to go and was able to go was approved. Thus, our chapter had a total of 16 delegates (including the nine from my agency) and three alternates who were set to go.

On Saturday morning, August 2000, seven of us boarded an American Airlines plane from Los Angeles International Airport to Washington, DC National Airport. I boarded first. I had a seat in first class using my frequent flyer miles. As each of the others boarded the flight, passing through first class, they said hello to me. The other passengers in first class were looking at me, trying to figure out who I was and why so many people were speaking to me. I got a kick out of this.

We arrived at National Airport. I had pre-arranged for a stretch limo to pick us up. Sure enough, a long white stretch limo was waiting for the entourage and we loaded up the trunk, packed into the limo and headed to the Marriott Wardman Park Hotel, the location for the 2000 Delegates Assembly and National Training Conference.

My chapter delegates were focused. We had one mission – to get me elected to the Board of Directors. Except for J. B. Larkins, none of us had ever attended a Delegates Assembly. We sat through the ordeal, met other Region IX delegates, and politely asked them to vote for me. We did not have to do a hard sell. We already had the votes. We just had to sit and relax until the voting began.

Gerald Reed, the National President was up for re-election. Opposing him was Oscar Eason, the previous National President, who had served for two terms (four years) and left because of term limits. Gerald Reed won the presidency with 374 votes representing 78.6% of the voting. Other National officers elected were Margaret Stephens as 1st Vice-President; Karen Griffin as 3rd Vice-President; and Arthur Henderson as Secretary.

Region IX had 33 voting delegates. I received 23 votes to my opponent's ten votes. I won the election with 69.7% of the vote. I had projected more delegates from Region IX and wanted to get twenty-eight votes or 75% of the votes. Nonetheless, I had defeated an incumbent and was newly elected to the National Board of Directors for 2001.

The Opening Plenary Session for the 2000 National Training Conference featured Congressman Jessie Jackson, Jr. as the keynote speaker. I attended the Department of Defense Agency Forum and after the session I went to the Press room and wrote an article on the Forum assisted by Dawn Lawson and Veronica Godfrey. The article appeared the next day in the Daily Update. My collaboration with Dawn and Veronica was the foundation of a long association. The conference ended with a Closing Plenary Session with former Congressman Ron Dellums as the keynote speaker.

Back in California, I continued to serve as chapter president. We produced the next issue of "BIG Connections" our quarterly newsletter. This issue featured the National Training Conference with articles written by chapter members attending the NTC and photos of members at the conference.

At the end of the year, I submitted an annual report to the chapter, highlighting our achievements and listing my presidential activities during the past year. Although, I still had a year on my term and could have remained president, I submitted my resignation as chapter president. I was looking forward to joining the National Board of Directors and making an impact at the national level.

Chapter 4: National Board 2001

"Leaders don't force people to follow – they invite them on a journey." – Charles S. Lauer

2001 was my first year on the Board. The first Board meeting was in Washington, DC. J. B. Larkins and I left together from Los Angeles International Airport. One of the first items on the agenda was the election of the Board Chair and Vice Chair. Ellen Dyson, the current Board Chair was challenged by Julius Crouch, a previous Board Chair. Ellen prevailed and won re-election for a third one-year term. The vote was eighteen to seven. John Lyons, from Region VIII, was re-elected as Vice Chair. Ellen made committee appointments and I was assigned to the Programs Oversight Committee, chaired by Daniel Corria.

By the second Board meeting in April, a situation was developing with the National Secretary. His behavior was bordering on being unprofessionalism in the way that he conducted himself both during and between meetings. I would have to monitor this developing situation.

The 2001 NTC was in Los Angeles, California. The host hotel was the St. Bonaventure. However, the Board stayed at the Downtown Marriott Hotel, a block away. The Conference was held at the Los Angeles Convention Center, about eight city blocks away. As part of the conference contract, the city provided buses to take attendees from their hotels to the convention center. During the NTC, most nights I drove home and slept in my own bed. The daily commute was 35 miles and leaving early in the morning, traffic was not bad.

The Closing Plenary session was in the afternoon at the Convention Center. During the Awards presentation, the Greater Los Angeles Federal Executive Board (FEB) received the Prestige Special Achievement Award. I had written the nomination and was very pleased that they received the award. I felt that this achievement would further solidify the relationship with the Federal Executive Board and the Los Angeles/Long Beach Area Chapter. Accepting the award was Kathrene Hansen, the Executive Director and Patricia Proctor, the FEB Office Secretary and a member of the Los Angeles/Long Beach Area Chapter.

On Saturday morning, prior to checkout time, several Board members were having breakfast at the Marriott Hotel, talking about the conference, the organization, and Board leadership, etc. It was a good conversation. I remembered saying something about my ideas of how the organization should evolve. Someone said, "Why don't you run for Board Chair?" I said that I'd consider it, if I had their support. There were about five other people there and they all kind of nodded their heads in a positive manner. I saw an opportunity.

After check-out, I drove immediately to my place of work in Los Alamitos, 25 miles away. There, I sent out e-mails to all the Board members and Executive Committee members announcing that I was running for the Chair of the National Board of Directors. I figured, correctly or not, that I had seven votes to start with and needed to get six more for the magic number of thirteen. I made the decision to run without consulting with my mentor, J.B. Larkins. Regardless, the race was on.

Chapter 5: First Year as Chair 2002

"Leadership is all about people. It is not about organization. It is not about plans. It is not about strategies. It is all about people – motivating people to get the job done. You have to be people-centered." – Colin Powell

Board Meeting; January 11, 2002; Embassy Suites; Kansas City, Missouri.

Immediately after I was sworn in as the Chair, the gavel was passed to me. I was now chairing the meeting. I announced that the next order of business was the adoption of the agenda. There is no transition time. Once elected, you must perform the duties of the Chair.

One of the duties of the Chair is to appoint the committee chairs with the approval of the Board. In reality, the Chair appoints the committee chairs and assigns the Board members to the committees. Basically, the action was without objection, even though some years, I did have challenges to both the committee chair appointments and committee assignments. But, I survived the challenges.

The election was over. My goal was to appoint the best people to the appropriate committees. I made the following committee chair appointments: Awards – Ellen Dyson; Constitution & Policy – Julius Crouch; Constitution & Policy, Policy – J. David Reeves; Constitution & Policy, By-laws – Cheryl Keitt; Financial Advisory Oversight – Oscar Williams; Personnel – Tommy Swanson: Program Oversight – Dan Corria; Strategic Planning – David Hampton; Time & Place/Delegates Assembly – C. Jacque Beatty; and an ad hoc committee, Facilities Acquisition – C. Jacque Beatty. I assigned other Board members to at least two committees. At 4:55 p.m. on January 11th, we recessed for committee meetings. The next day, Saturday, January 12th, we reconvened at 9:12 a.m. We continued to conduct the business of the organization. For lunch, we were transported to Gates, a famous barbeque restaurant in Kansas City, and enjoyed delicious ribs with Gates own brand of barbeque sauce.

The Board approved several actions during the meeting. Some of the significant ones included authorization for the Time & Place Committee to solicit bids for the 2004 National Training Conference; approval of the nomination procedures for a National Board Member Recognition Award. During my five years as Board Chair, I never recognized any Board member for this award. I was against it. Instead, each year I recognized all Board members with a gift, fitting for display on their desk, that had their name inscribed on it and the year of service. On a motion by the Personnel Committee, we approved the revised Personnel Manual; approved starting salaries for the Accounts Payable Specialist and the Accountant; and approved performance bonuses for the National Office Staff.

Just before the Board adjourned, I made the following remarks, "First, thank you David Hampton for being a super host for us. I've really enjoyed myself. I especially enjoyed the barbeque, etc. Also, I want to thank everyone for assisting me in my learning curve and it's been a unique experience for me because I did some talking at the meeting for a change."

There was laughter. Why? Because during the whole year of 2001, I never made a motion, nor spoke on any motions or issues. Other than self introductions at the start of some meetings, the most I had ever said was "Present" during roll calls. So, constantly speaking throughout the meeting was unusual and a new experience for me and everyone else listening. I actually overheard someone say, "He can talk".

The meeting adjourned at 9:17 p.m. on Saturday, January 12, 2002.

Board Meeting; May 3, 2002; Marriott Wardman Park Hotel; Washington, DC.

The meeting was called to order at 8:30 a.m. We had roll call, approved the agenda, and proceeded with the order of business. At 1:00 pm. we recessed to journey to the new National headquarters located on

Georgia Avenue, NW, Washington, D.C. for the Ribbon-cutting Ceremony. The event was well-attended. Margaret Stephens, the 1st Vice President served as Mistress of Ceremonies. During the program, I made remarks and introduced each member of the Board of Directors. Joining us at the ceremony was U.S. Congresswoman Eleanor Holmes Norton, representative for the District of Columbia. Congresswoman Holmes Norton had always been a strong supporter of BIG and was the keynote speaker at our first National Training Conference in 1978. With Sylvia Johnson Herring, Assistant Treasurer and Dawn Lawson, National Secretary, holding the ribbon on each end and me standing to the right of Dawn Lawson and Congresswoman Holmes Norton and Gerald Reed, National President, standing in the middle with scissors in hand, the ribbon was cut and Blacks In Government was introduced to its new neighbors and welcomed to the community. After the ribbon cutting, attendees went on a tour of the building and reception where refreshments were served.

On Saturday morning, May 4th, I officially re-convened the meeting to order at 8:47 a.m. and thanked everyone present for showing up at 8:45 a.m. After roll call, it was determined that we did not have a quorum, so I announced a recess for ten minutes. During my time as Board Chair, it was always a struggle to get Board members to come to the meetings on time. Some had valid reasons and others did not.

Finally, we got a quorum and the meeting proceeded. When we arrived to the part on the agenda to fill a Board vacancy, I announced that I had received correspondence from Mr. John Lyons, Region VIII, resigning effective January the 27th, due to a relocation of his job to Taiwan. I also received correspondence from the Regional Council of Region VIII, stating in a special meeting that they had recommended a replacement for Mr. Lyons and that replacement was Ms. Greta D. Jones-Sanders.

According to the Constitution of Blacks In Government the Board Chair appoints the vacancies on the Board of Directors. So exercising that power, I recommended the appointment of Ms. Greta Jones-Sanders to fill the vacant position and term of Mr. John Lyons. All I needed was for the Board to confirm the act. Mr. Crouch moved to ratify my recommended appointment. Mr. Larkins seconded the motion. The motion passed. Ms. Greta Jones-Sanders was appointed the Region VIII Director.

This was a very long meeting. There were a lot of issues and motions. There were plenty of discussion and a lot of debate. There were a lot of "hot air" and plenty of personal agendas.

By the conclusion of the meeting, the Board had approved several Policy Manual changes; approved the Awards Committee's recommendations of the BIG Prestige Awards: for the Meritorious Service Award – Mary K. Thomas, BIG Pentagon Chapter, Region XI; for the Distinguished Service Award – the Los Angeles/Long Beach Area Chapter; and for the Special Achievement Award – the Department of Labor Choir, Region XI. The Board approved the by-laws of seventeen chapters; approved the reallocation of certain budget line items; approved the charters of twelve interest groups; approved the hiring of the full-time accountant; approved the learning center at the National headquarters be named after Janice M. Scott; and approved a special award for Mr. Claiborne Haughton upon his retirement as the Director of the Civil Rights for the Department of Defense.

The meeting did not adjourn until 2:08 a.m. on Sunday morning, May 5th. I was tired and had to leave early the same morning on a flight back to California. The second meeting that I chaired was too long (for me). For others, it was just like old times. Never again. Fingers crossed.

J. B. Larkins and I left Los Angeles International Airport on Thursday morning, August 22, 2002 for Atlanta, Georgia to attend the Board of Directors meeting, Delegates Assembly, and the 24th Annual National Training Conference. We boarded the early American Airlines flight, with a transfer in Dallas, and arrived at Hartsfield Atlanta International Airport. On October 20, 2003, Atlanta's City Council changed the name from Hartsfield Atlanta International Airport to the current Hartsfield-Jackson Atlanta International Airport, in honor of former mayor Maynard Jackson, the first African-American mayor of Atlanta, who died on June 23, 2003.

We proceeded to the baggage claim area and met our limousine driver for the ride to the Atlanta Hilton Hotel. The drive was approximately twenty minutes. I checked into the hotel and went to my room, which was the Presidential Suite on the top floor. Actually the suite was two floors with stairs to the upper level where the sleeping area and the Jacuzzi was located.

The Board met on Thursday evening for our customary "Round Table Discussions" and I welcomed everyone to Atlanta. As Board Chair, I was responsible for presenting the Board's annual report to the Delegates Assembly. I had prepared the report and arranged for the Kinko's located at the hotel to print six hundred copies. The copies were needed by Friday for volunteers to place them in the Delegates Assembly bags.

Board Meeting; August 23, 2002; Atlanta Hilton Hotel; Atlanta, Georgia.

I called the meeting to order at 9:27 a.m. After the opening prayer, we established a quorum and acknowledged the visitors at the meeting. We approved an amended agenda and proceeded to conduct the business of the organization.

One of the first items on the agenda was the report and recommendations of the Constitution & Policy, Constitution Committee. Each year, the Board must consider all the constitutional amendments proposals and make recommendations to the Delegates Assembly whether to "adopt" or "not adopt". Sometimes the Board agrees with the recommendations of the Constitution & Policy, Constitution Committee and sometimes it doesn't. We had heated debates on what we wanted to present or recommend to the Delegates Assembly.

After acting on the proposed amendments, the Board needed to approve any new chapter charters. There were four interest groups up for approval – the Denver Federal Center from Region VIII; BIG at the Crossroads and the Washington D.C. Black Caucus from Region XI;

the Liberty interest group from Region III. Once the interest groups were approved for their charters, the By-Laws Committee had to prepare their charters for my signature and I had to prepare a memorandum for the Delegates Assembly Chair to provide to the Credentials Committee should the new chapters have delegates at the National Delegates Assembly.

The Board received the President's Report; Treasurer's Report to include the Audit Report for review; Regional Directors' Reports; and Board Committees' Reports. The Time and Place/Delegates Assembly recommended that the 2004 National Training Conference of Blacks In Government be held in Washington, DC. The recommendation was approved by the Board. I made the announcement in the Delegates Assembly.

After meeting for two days, the Board recessed at 7:40 p.m. on Saturday, August 24, 2002 (subject to call by the Board Chair).

National Delegates Assembly

The 2002 National Delegates Assembly was a Presidential election year for BIG. That election was the highlight of the Assembly. I sat on the platform, next to Gerald Reed, the National President. I introduced each member of the Board of Directors; presented new chapters with their charters, requested the ratification for revoking chapters in compliance with the organization's financial reporting requirements, and then I made my first speech before this esteemed body. The Board of Directors' 2002 Annual Report to the Delegates was already in the delegates' possession, so I gave a summary of its contents. Contained in the report were significant successes: (1) our support for the passage of the Notification of Federal Employee Anti-discrimination Retaliation Act "No Fear". A BIG representative attended the bill signing at the White House on May 15, 2002 and a photo appeared in an issue of Jet Magazine; (2) the purchase of our new National Headquarters at 3005 Georgia Avenue, NW in Washington, D.C.; (3) BIG selected as one of the 100+ Influential Organizations and featured in the May issue of Ebony Magazine; and (4) approval for participation in the Combined Federal Campaign (CFC) as a designated voluntary charitable organization.

When the time came for questions and answers, I was asked only one question and that was by Ms. Rubye Fields. The delegates gave me a 'bye'. That was the first and only time that they did. I was relieved. I was not comfortable standing in front of over 600 people in the audience. I had survived my first Delegates Assembly.

Running for President were a record six qualified individuals. Rawle King was the Region XI Council President; J. David Reeves was the Vice-Chair of the National Board of Directors and former 1st Vice-President; Gregg Reeves was the National Executive Vice-President and former member of the Board of Directors; Oscar Eason was a former National President and former Chair of the National Board of Directors; Larry Harris was a former 3rd Vice-President and former member of the Board of Directors; Howard Ervin was a former member of the Board of Directors and former President of the Region VI Council.

No one had a clear majority of the votes on the first ballot and there was a run-off between J. David Reeves and Gregg Reeves, the two leading vote getters. Ultimately, Gregg Reeves won the election with 345 votes (57.9%) to J. David Reeves' 250 votes (42.1%).

The Board of Directors elections results were interesting. Seven incumbents were re-elected; one incumbent defeated; and three decided not to run for re-election. Four incumbents ran unopposed and one new candidate was not opposed. Of the three incumbents that ran opposed their winning percentages were 59.2%; 72.7%; and 64.0%. The incumbent that lost was defeated by 71.1% of the vote. The four new board members for 2003 were Johnita (Jackie) Pitts, Region III, Dr Doris Sartor, Region IV, Katherine Cage, Region VI, and Charles Oliver, Region X.

Other National officers elected were Margaret Stephens, 1st Vice President; Karen Griffin, 3rd Vice-President; Dawn Lawson, National Secretary; and Faye Stewart-Henderson, Treasurer.

Board Meeting; November 16, 2002; Marriott Marquis Hotel; Atlanta, Georgia

The Board gathered in Atlanta, along with the Executive Committee, for a joint session to begin our work on developing a strategic plan for the organization. We worked on the document on Friday and most of Saturday, November 15th & 16th. Mr. J.D. McConnell from the Army's Command & General Staff College Center for Leadership at Fort Leavenworth, Kansas and his wife, Dr. Mary McConnell served as facilitators. We agreed on the organization's mission, vision and values. We also set in place some short-term action items associated with each objective. The session was very productive. I believe we all walked away with a sense of accomplishment. Having a strategic plan identifies who you are and what you're about. I am often asked by prospective members about our strategic plan. I belong to other organizations and one of the tell-tale signs when it comes to the structure of these organizations is a strategic plan or lack of one. The Board of Directors got to interact with members of the Executive Committee and vice versa. We participated in several exercises with the purpose of strengthening the team concept.

I called the Board of Directors' meeting to order on Saturday afternoon, November 16, 2002 at 4:30 p.m. The major item on the agenda was the approval of the 2003 budget. We increased the registrations fees for NTC 2003. We approved a revision of the Prestige Awards criteria; approved changes and added a new policy to the Policy Manual; approved several chapter by-laws and the chartering of a chapter. We also approved the payment of the initial profit share of $25,000 to the Region IV Council within the next 30 days since more than 90 percent of post conference activities had been completed.

During our "good of the order", Charlie Hampton, Region X, shared the following, "Fellow Board members, I want an opportunity to say good-bye to you guys personally in this forum. I mean. I've been here for six years. I came in a neophyte. I'm leaving having learned a lot about the organization. I've enjoyed working with all of you who are still here. Some have passed and some who are leaving with me. But I think the most important thing for me is I have watched the Board as an organization grow in terms of the expertise and the strength, and also how it uses its time. When I first came here, we were spending two and a half days, midnight, 2:00 o'clock in the morning. Now we're down to about a day, day and a half. And I think as you keep going, you'll probably have it down to less than a day. Take care of business like business is supposed to be taken care of, and have committees that function, committees that function the way they should function. So I commend you on the progress. And who knows, I might be back one day. But as Carol said, "I will be watching also."

Just before we adjourned, I took the opportunity to say, "It is 11:30 p.m. We started at 4:30 p.m. We ended at 11:30 p.m. Seven hours. Thank you very much".

The Board would not meet again until next year.

Immediately, after my return home, the next item on my agenda was the preparation of my re-election campaign. I started strategizing who my possible opponents would be and how many "beans" votes that I thought I had. Carolyn Adams, a member of the Los Angeles/Long Beach Area Chapter provided me with Kwanzaa cards to send to the Board members. I contacted key communicators asking them to make phone calls to Board members at appropriate times and I established timelines for when I would send e-mails and make phone calls. I mailed each member a gift for their service on the Board that year. I used a piece of campaign literature designed by the grandson (a 7th grader) of a friend and hoped that it was worth two votes. I thought there might be five candidates for the position of Chair. In the end, there were four of us vying for the position. My focus was on winning. That's what I proceeded to do.

Chapter 6: Repeat as Chair 2003

"The single biggest way to impact an organization is to focus on leadership development. There is almost no limit to the potential of an organization that recruits good people, raises them up as leaders and continually develops them." – John C. Maxwell

Blacks In Government
National Board of Directors Meeting
Marriott Wardman Park Hotel
Washington, DC
Friday, January 17, 2003

Excerpts from the official transcript:

Mr. Farrell Chiles: The National Board of Directors meeting is now called to order. It is 9:37 a.m., on January 17th, 2003.

We would like to start the meeting off with an opening prayer. And Mr. Walton, will you lead us in prayer....

Mr. Farrell Chiles: Thank you. Next item on the agenda is the election of Board Chair and Vice-Chair. Again, I turn the meeting over to Mr. Walton.

Mr. Thomas Walton: This morning we will be assisted by M. Peggy Downing, Mr. Rawle King, Ms. Faye Stewart-Henderson, and Ms. Angela Harvey. Again, I refer you to Article VI of the National Constitution of Blacks In Government, Section 1-B. "Chair of the Board Directors serves as the Chair of the Board of Directors, officially transmits the policies which have been approved by the Board of Directors, recommends to the Board of Directors changes in policies and procedures, presents the organization's annual report to the annual Delegates Assembly, appoints committee chairs of the board with the consent of the board, and is an ex-officio member of the board committees.

Requires reports on the activities of the Regional Councils and the chapters through the Board of Directors from the regions and board committees. Performs such functions and exercises such other activities as may be prescribed by the Board of Directors. The Chair of the board cannot be a member of the Executive Committee." Any questions?

(No response)

Mr. Thomas Walton: We're going to ask, Ms. Harvey, if you record the names of those whose names may be placed for nomination for the office of Chair of the National Board of Directors. At this time we declare the floor open for nominations for Chair of the National Board of Directors, Blacks In Government. The Chair recognizes Mr. Larkins.

Mr. J.B. Larkins: J.B. Larkins, Region IX. I nominate Mr. Farrell Chiles.

Mr. Thomas Walton: Farrell Chiles has been nominated. The Chair recognizes Ms. David Hampton.

Ms. David Hampton: Mr. Chair, I nominate Julius Crouch.

Mr. Thomas Walton: Mr. Julius Crouch has been nominated. Any further nominations?...Mr. Oliver.

Mr. Charles Oliver: I nominate Mr. Remond Henderson.

Mr. Thomas Walton: Mr. Remond Henderson has been nominated. Are there any further nominations for the office of Chair of the National Board of Directors? Ms. Ellen Dyson.

Ms. Ellen Dyson: I nominate Mr. J. David Reeves.

Mr. Thomas Walton: Mr. J. David Reeves has been nominated. Are there any further nominations for the office of Chair of the National Board of Directors, second call?

(No response)

Mr. Thomas Walton: On third and final call, are there any further nominations for the office of Chair… Seeing no hands, hearing no voices, the Chair declares the nominations closed on the names of Farrell Chiles, Julius Crouch, Remond Henderson, and J. David Reeves for the office of Chair of the National Board of Directors of Blacks In Government…At this time we will hear from each of the candidates. We will begin with Mr. Farrell Chiles…Three minutes at the max.

Mr. Farrell Chiles: First, I want to thank you for allowing me to serve as your Chair of the Board of Directors this past year. I want you to know that I sincerely appreciate each and every one for your time, talents, and contributions to this organization.

I am glad to stand before you again today, asking for your support in me again this year as your Board Chair. As we begin the Year 2003, I smell a scent of newness and opportunities for us to embrace the many changes and challenges that we have before us.

For me, I am committed to this organization's dreams. My pledge is to take BIG to even a higher level by collaborating with the National Executive Committee and truly conducting ourselves as one team, assisting in corporate fund-raising activities to strengthen our financial base, increasing membership by encouraging and advising and coaching prospective new members, to initiate new chapters within the state and municipal sectors in the United States, Virgin Islands, and abroad and continuing to improve Board operations in our decision making process.

You know, each of us has an overflow of attributes that would enable BIG to grow and soar. We are member-focused, determined, and energetic, performance driven and goal-oriented leaders. With that, I believe that the future is bright for Blacks In Government.

So I ask you to dream BIG and endorse me as the Chair of the Board of Directors. Vote for me, Farrell Chiles, for Board Chair. Thank you again.

(Applause)

Mr. Thomas Walton: Thank you, Mr. Chiles. The Chair recognizes Mr. Julius Crouch. Three minutes.

Mr. Julius Crouch: I come before you this morning asking that you allow me the privilege and opportunity to serve the coming year as your Board Chair. Why? I'm knowledgeable, I'm experienced, I'm committed.

There are some other reasons, too. We're talking about improving effectiveness and efficiency. I think the improvement of that effectiveness and efficiency needs to start right here with the Board. If we're going to lead we need to improve what we're doing and there are some things that we need to change.

We need to complete the strategic plan because not just this year, but as we look out into the future, we need to get that plan completed and implemented. Financial viability. I'm going to say to you – that's a little bit more – we're that far from bankruptcy. One major failure and we're in bankruptcy, folks. We need to do some things different from the way we've done them in the past. We need to take some extreme steps to change the way things are going.

And last, but by no means least, we need to address those issues and situations that are impacting each and every one of us and our constituency and our members at home.

I ask that you vote for Julius Crouch as your Chair and request that you allow me to serve you for the next year as Chair of the Board. Thank you very much.

(Applause)

Mr. Thomas Walton: The Chair recognizes Remond Henderson, Region X. Three minutes.

Mr. Remond Henderson: Thank you, Mr. Chair. I would like to use one minute of my time to ask each or you to pull out the document that I passed out, one page, with Vote for Remond Henderson. Of all the paperwork that you get, it's probably buried. I'd like for you to pull it out and ask you to read it. I'm going to use one minute of my time to ask you to read that document.

(Members complied)

Mr. Remond Henderson: The speed readers are done. Well, this document speaks for itself and it addresses my experiences and addresses the things I'd like to focus on; but primarily, you are the ones that set the direction. The job of the Board Chair is to administratively conduct the meetings and accomplish the items on the agenda.

I've got the experience as an administrator, as a Chair, as a person that presides over meetings, and that's what I bring to the table.

I'm no more articulate than Mr. Crouch or any other candidate, but I do, I think, bring to this table administrative experience as well as financial experience; and I would look forward to serving as your Board Chair, and I solicit your support. Thank you.

(Applause)

Mr. Thomas Walton: The Chair recognizes Mr. J. David Reeves. Three minutes.

Mr. J. David Reeves: Good morning. I think you all know that I am skilled in this area. As a trained parliamentarian, I do have the capability and knowledge to conduct the meetings in an appropriate fashion. I think you also know that I am not one who is shy to make a decision. I'm straightforward. I'm honest. And I'm direct.

I've received the support of a number of people who have expressed an interest in someone taking the helm who they believe will move forward in a direction of making positive change for the organization. You all know that I ran for president of this organization, and in a run-off election I lost. However, my good colleague and friend, Gregg Reeves – and I don't know where the misnomer came that Gregg and I are not friends. Gregg and I are extremely close and have spoken on a number of occasions since that time and have visions that, as a team, that we can work together, with the Board and Executive Committee coinciding in a positive direction that people of this organization, we believe, will find not only will be a benefit of Blacks In Government but taking this organization to new heights and new directions.

I have the experience. I have the knowledge. I have the background. I have the desire. I have the passion, and I have the dreams. I simply ask that you look inside your heart and recognize that there is more to running a Board than just wanting to do the position; but it is about preparing yourself with the necessary skills, which I have done not only with Blacks In Government, but organizations around the country.

I love this organization. I continue to struggle. I continue to fight. And I think I have what it takes to take this Board to new heights and new directions. And I ask for your vote for Chair of the Board. Thank you.

(Applause)

Mr. Thomas Walton: The ballots that you're going to be presented are the ballots for the Chair of the National Board of Directors. It says election ballot. IT also says got for only one candidate. Please print clearly. The names are on the board. There can be no write-in names. All right?...

Mr. Thomas Walton: Let the record show that 24 ballots have been collected. Ms. Henderson, would you now start reading names, and Ms. Harvey will record the number…

Ms. Stewart-Henderson:
Remond Henderson.
Remond Henderson.
Remond Henderson.
Farrell Chiles
Farrell Chiles
Remond Henderson.
Farrell Chiles.
Mr. Julius Crouch.
Farrell Chiles.
J. David Reeves.
J. David Reeves.
Julius Crouch.
J. David Reeves.
J. David Reeves.
Farrell Chiles.
J. David Reeves.
Julius Crouch.
J. David Reeves.
J. David Reeves.
Farrell Chiles.
Farrell Chiles.
Farrell Chiles.
Farrell Chiles.
And last, J. David Reeves.

Mr. Thomas Walton: Let the record show that Farrell Chiles has received 9 votes. Mr. Julius Crouch, 3. Mr. Remond Henderson, 4. Mr. J. David Reeves, 8. In order to be elected, it would take thirteen votes or a majority over the twenty-four. Therefore, we will have a run-off election for the office of Chairman of the Board of Directors, Mr. Farrell Chiles and Mr. J. David Reeves.

Mr. Thomas Walton: Let the record show that the Regional Director from Region II, Mr. Merton Simpson, has arrive in the room…he is an eligible Board member to vote…

Mr. Thomas Walton: There are 25 ballots that have been collected. At this time would your read. And Mr. King would your verify as Ms Henderson reads, please.

Ms. Stewart-Henderson:

J. David Reeves.

Reeves.

Farrell Chiles.

J. David Reeves.

Farrell Chiles.

Farrell Chiles.

Farrell Chiles.

Farrell Chiles.

J. David Reeves.

J. David Reeves.

J. David Reeves.

Farrell Chiles.

J. David Reeves.

Farrell Chiles.

J. David Reeves.

Farrell Chiles

Farrell Chiles.

J. David Reeves.

J. David Reeves.

Farrell Chiles.

Farrell Chiles.

Farrell Chiles.

Farrell Chiles.

Farrell Chiles.

And lastly, Farrell Chiles.

Mr. Thomas Walton: Let the record show that Mr. Farrell Chiles received fifteen votes. Mr. J. David Reeves has received ten votes.

The Chair, therefore, declares Mr. Farrell Chiles re-elected as the Chairman of the National Board of Directors of Blacks In Government.

(Applause)

J. David Reeves was re-elected as Vice-Chair.

We completed the election process at 10:40 a.m. and then took a 15 minute break

Prior to the election of the Board Chair and Vice Chair, the Board approved my appointment of Howard Ervin to fill the unexpired term of Faye Stewart-Henderson as Region VI's Regional Director.

The Board also approved the President's appointment of Ms. Cynthia Davis as National Secretary to fill the vacancy left by Ms. Dawn Lawson.

Also joining the Board was the new National President, Gregg Reeves. Gregg's first action items were the Board's approval of Charlene Lee as the Executive Vice President and Walt Washington as Second Vice-President. Both were approved. Mr. Reeves submitted names for the standing committees and all were approved.

During the meeting, I announced my appointments for the Board's committee chairs.

Awards: Ellen Dyson.

Constitution & Policy: Julius Crouch.

Constitution & Policy, Constitution: Julius Crouch.

Constitution & Policy, Policy: Howard Ervin.

Constitution & Policy, By-laws: Cheryl Keitt.

Financial Advisory Oversight: Oscar Williams.

Personnel: Greta Jones-Sanders.

Strategic Planning: Ms. David Hampton.

Time & Place/Delegates Assembly: C. Jacquie Beatty.

Facility Acquisition: C. Jacquie Beatty.

I tried to put four people on each of the committees and attempted to ensure that no one was serving on more than two committees.

During the two days of meeting, the Board approved to suspend eighteen chapters for non-compliance of financial reporting. We approved the by-laws of five chapters and the charter of one new chapter. We approved a change to the life membership installment payment plan. The Board approved the firm of Bert Smith & Company as our auditors. We approved the expenditure of funds for the purchase of office equipment and furniture. We decided to hold our spring Board meeting in Las Vegas, Nevada and the fall meeting in Memphis, Tennessee.

The Board went into Executive Session for a presentation by Mr. Ron Jessamy, our outside attorney, who brought us up to date on our legal issues and pending lawsuits.

Before entertaining a motion for adjournment, I made the following statement, "I would like to thank my fellow Board members for your confidence in me and in selecting me again as this year's Chair of the Board. I pledge to you that I will continue to improve, and I appreciate the mentoring, the guidance, the support, and I look forward to a very productive year."

Board of Directors Meeting; April 11, 2003; Las Vegas Marriott Suites; Las Vegas, Nevada

I drove to Las Vegas – 245 miles from my house – three and one half hours away - for the meeting.

On Thursday evening, during the "Round Table Discussions," we had a presentation from the City of Detroit, who was interested in hosting a future National Training Conference. A representative from the MGM in Las Vegas also made a presentation. At the end of each presentation, Board members received nice gifts on behalf of the cities.

At the Board meeting the next morning, we received greetings from Mr. Oscar Webb, founder of Blacks In Gaming and the former president of the National Gaming Organization.

We then conducted the business of Blacks In Government. The Board adjourned at 5:12 p.m. on Saturday evening. Most members were in a rush to finish the meeting, because we had received complimentary tickets to attend a David Copperfield event at the MGM Hollywood Theater at 7:00 p.m. that evening. I did not attend. The next morning, I drove home. Our next Board meeting would be in Denver, Colorado just prior to the National Training Conference.

In July 2003, I attended the Urban League's Annual Conference in Pittsburgh, Pennsylvania. I stayed at the Hilton Hotel and took the chartered bus to the convention center every day. One morning I sat next to a gentleman named Carl Dickerson of Dickerson Employee Benefits was the former Vice-Chair of the Los Angeles Urban League Board of Directors. We exchanged pleasantries and I told him that I was the Chairman of the Board of Blacks In Government and was a member of the Los Angeles/Long Beach Area Chapter. I told him about the Scholarship program and we exchanged business cards. Upon my return to Los Angeles, I sent him a letter requesting a contribution to the scholarship program and he responded with a check for $1,000.00.

I had met Otis Mills, President of the Greater Pittsburgh Chapter at the 2000 National Training Conference in Washington, DC. He had attended the Officer Leadership Training of which I was a presenter. I called Otis and told him that I would be in Pittsburgh for the National Urban League Conference and he had given me his cell phone to make contact. Otis worked for the Department of Energy in Pittsburgh and his agency was an exhibitor at the conference. We arranged to get together one evening and he drove me to his home to meet his family. We had great conversation and Otis shared with me his chapter's accomplishments including a very successful chapter training conference conducted at the Pittsburgh Federal Building in February 2003. We decided to have dinner at Simmies, a local seafood restaurant. Otis informed me that he had invited Ms. Rebecca Lewis, the chapter's Vice-President to join us, along with his wife.

We had great conversation and the food was delicious. While at dinner, I talked about my role as Chairman of the Board, the requirements of the position, and my need for an Executive Assistant. I was impressed with Rebecca Lewis' conversation, disposition, and the manner in which she presented herself. Rebecca's first attendance at a

National Training Conference was in Atlanta in 2002. I suggested that she should attend the next one in Denver and consider serving as my Executive Assistant. Within a week of my return to California, I received an e-mail from Rebecca stating that she would accept the position. I was very pleased with her decision to assist me.

2003 National Training Conference; Adams Mark Hotel; Denver, Colorado

I arrived at the Denver Airport and after retrieving my luggage, I was escorted to a holding room where the Conference Hospitality Committee had arranged for food and beverages and transportation to the conference hotel in downtown Denver. The Board met at 7:00 p.m. that evening for our traditional "Round Table Discussions" session. We met the next morning (Friday) for the Board meeting.

Rebecca Lewis, my new Executive Assistant arrived on Saturday and upon her arrival, we became a team. We gelled immediately. Every morning, we would start the day with coffee in my suite and then tackle the agenda for the day. Unless there was a luncheon that I had to attend, we had lunch together at the same hotel restaurant. I always ordered a bowl of chicken noodle soup and Rebecca usually had a salmon salad.

Richard Shields, the Conference Chair, had arranged to have a luncheon recognizing youth. I partnered with him and came up with the title "The Chairman's Tribute to Youth". We had certificates of appreciation designed to present to six outstanding students. I further worked with Shirley Harrington, the Legislative Affairs Committee Chair, and she assured us that attendees from her Governance in America Special Emphasis Program would attend the youth luncheon. Shirley was able to obtain corporate funding to defray the cost of the luncheon and thus allow for maximum attendance. The event was very successful and was the forerunner of the scholarship awards at the next year's National Training Conference.

At the Closing Plenary Session, Kimberly Best-Tuten, my first Executive Assistant, received the coveted BIG Meritorious Service Award. She had sent me a draft of the nomination in early February for my review and I was very happy that she had won the award. Her mother was at the event and that made it very special for her. I had known since April that she was the winner but I had not informed her. It's Board protocol that we do not reveal the winners until the announcement at the Closing Plenary Session.

Board of Directors Meeting; October 31, 2003; Marriott Hotel Downtown; Memphis, Tennessee

The meeting was called to order at 9:13 a.m. Mr. Thomas Walton led all assembled with an opening prayer. In the prayer, he acknowledged the absence of our transcriber, Ms. Marlene Martin Kerr, who was unable to attend the meeting because she was on bed rest (having a baby). Substituting for her was her twin sister, Ms. Arlene Martin Malone.

We received a greeting from Ms. Linda Kelly, President of the Greater Memphis Chapter; The County Mayor, the Honorable A.C. Wharton, Jr.; and Mr. Hugh Davis, BIG Life Member, Senior Executive Service (SES) and IRS Director of Field Services.

We went around the room and had introductions, established a quorum, approved the amended agenda, and went about the business of Blacks In Government.

During the President's Report, on behalf of the National Executive Committee, a motion was considered to hold the Delegates Assembly on Saturday and Sunday prior to the start of the annual National Training Conference. The results of a survey conducted revealed that six regions were against changing the days and five were for the change. After discussing the pros and cons and weighing the impact of the change, the motion failed. The Board approved the appointment of Ms. Loverna Miller as Communications and Public Relations Chair for the National Organization.

The Board approved a recommendation by the Constitution & Policy Committee (Policy) pertaining to Policy 1:41, subject: Fundraising. The first sentence in the motion clarified that "the National Board of Directors shall be responsible for fund-raising policies and procedures for the National Organization."

Also at the meeting were the newly-elected Board members whose term would start in January 2004. They had arrived a day early for new Board member orientation. The question arose as to whether we should permit them to sit at the Board table. Traditionally, only the Board members, the parliamentarian, and transcriber sit at the table during the meeting. A motion was made to have the future Board members sit at a table placed on the side of the Board's table. The motion passed.

Other actions approved by the Board included:

- Accepted the Treasurer's report for information only.
- Accepted the FY 2204 budget recommendations as proposed by the Financial Advisory Oversight Committee.
- Approved a cost of living increase for the National Office staff at the lesser of four percent or the cost of living index in the Washington, D.C. metropolitan area.'
- Accepted the Strategic Plan 2002 as a base document to proceed forth.
- Accepted the implementation of the Organization Strategic Plan process.
- Approved the by-laws and revised by-laws of eight chapters.
- Approved the chartering of the Gaithersburg DOC/NIST interest groups.
- Directed the National President to provide the membership on BIG's effort in addressing a revision to the new EEOC Management Directive 715.

The meeting adjourned on Saturday, November 1, 2003 at 4:43 p.m.

That evening, we were transported to the Stax Museum of American Soul Music, located at the original site of the legendary Stax Records "in the heart of Soulsville USA in Memphis, Tennessee." The Memphis Visitors Bureau had arranged for a reception at the Museum. We met local dignitaries, went on a tour of the museum, and enjoyed the delicious food and fine wine. Many of the Board members purchased memorabilia and gifts while there.

Chapter 7: Three Repeat 2004

"The key to successful leadership today is influence, not authority." – Kenneth Blanchard

Blacks In Government
National Board of Directors Meeting
Embassy Suites Hotel
San Diego, California
Friday, January 30, 2004

Excerpts from the official transcript:

Mr. Farrell Chiles: Good morning. Today is Friday, January 30, 2004. The time is 9:15 a.m. The Board of Directors' meeting of Blacks In Government is now in session.

I would like everyone to stand and I would like Mr. Walton to lead us in prayer....

Mr. Farrell Chiles: Moving right ahead, the next item on the agenda, item number six is the election of the Board Chair and Vice Chair: and I again yield to Mr. Walton to conduct the election.

Mr. Thomas Walton: In accordance with Article VI, Section 1 of the National Constitution of Blacks In Government, under National Officers, Chair of the Board of Directors, the Chair shall serve as the Chair of the Board of Directors, transmits the policies which have been approved by the Board of Directors, recommends to the Board of Directors changes in policies and procedures, presents the organization's annual report to the annual Delegates Assembly, appoints committee chairs of the board with the consent of the board, and is an ex-officio member of the board committees.

Requires reports on the activities of the Regional Councils and the chapters through the Board of Directors from the regions and board committees. Performs such functions and exercises such other activities as may be prescribed by the Board of Directors. The Chair of the board cannot be a member of the Executive Committee…

In accordance with the Policy Manual of the National Board of Directors, Policy 3:07, Election of the Board Chair, the election of the Chair and Vice Chair of the Board of Directors shall be by secret ballot with the majority vote for the election unless there is but one nomination for the Chair or Vice Chair, in which case the election shall be by acclamation.

If there is not one elected on the first ballot, then the two candidates with the highest number of votes for the Chair or Vice Chair will participate in a run-off election for their respective position.

Nominations shall be from the floor. The term of the office for the Chair and Vice Chair shall be for one year or until their successors are elected. The term of office shall begin immediately following the election. The effective date of this policy [is] 9 January 1993, Board of Directors meeting…

Ms. David Hampton: Mr. Parliamentarian.

Mr. Thomas Walton: Yes, ma'am.

Ms. David Hampton: I would like to offer a motion as to the structure of the election of the Chair and Vice Chair of the Board.

Mr. Thomas Walton: Yes, ma'am.

Ms. David Hampton: I move that the 2004 election of the National Board of Directors, Chair and Vice Chair, include a presentation of each candidate not to exceed five minutes and a period not to exceed fifteen minutes of question and answer of a panel of candidates for each office.

Mr. Charles Oliver: I second that motion.

Mr. Farrell Chiles: It's been moved by Ms. Hampton, seconded by Mr. Oliver that the 2004 election of the National Board of Directors, Chair and Vice Chair, include a presentation of each candidate not to exceed five minutes and a period not to exceed fifteen minutes of question and answer of a panel of candidates for each office. Discussion?

Ms. Jacquie Beatty: I have a question. Should this motion pass, say, for instance, we nominate someone who isn't here and will not be able to participate in this five minute thing, right, that's correct, so that person would be ineligible? Is that what we're saying?

Mr. Farrell Chiles: The motion doesn't state that.

Ms. Jacquie Beatty: I'm just trying to get clarity.

Mr. Farrell Chiles: They would not be able to make a presentation or participate in the question and answer session.

Ms. Jacquie Beatty: But that doesn't eliminate them as a candidate?

Mr. Farrell Chiles: That's correct.

Ms. Jacquie Beatty: Thank you.

Mr. Farrell Chiles: Mr. Browne.

Mr. Ralph Browne: Ralph Browne, Region I. Therefore, for purposes of clarification, a person does not have to make his platform known and that will not disqualify him or anything. And on the second part, the fifteen minutes – it doesn't have to be fifteen minutes; it can be drawn to a close before the fifteen minutes if there are no questions?

Mr. Farrell Chiles: It says not to exceed.

Ms. David Hampton: Not to exceed.

Mr. Ralph Browne: Okay; just for clarification.

Mr. Farrell Chiles: Other discussion?

(No response)

Mr. Farrell Chiles: All those in favor of the motion, say aye. (Members complied).

Mr. Farrell Chiles: Opposed, nay.

(No response)

Mr. Farrell Chiles: Motion carried. Mr. Walton….

Mr. Thomas Walton: We, therefore, declare for the record that there are 22 eligible voters who are members of the National Board of Directors who are present on this date in January 2004 for this election and nomination process.

At this time the Chair opens the floor for nominations for the office of the Chairman of the National Board of Directors of Blacks In Government.

Mr. J.B. Larkins: Mr. Chairman, J.B. Larkins, Region IX. I nominate Farrell Chiles.

Mr. Thomas Walton: Farrell Chiles has been nominated. On second call, the floor is open for the nominations for the office of Chairman of the National Board of Directors. Recognizing Mr. Oliver.

Mr. Charles Oliver: Yes, Mr. Chair, Charles Oliver, Region X. I want to nominate Mr. Remond Henderson.

Mr. Thomas Walton: Mr. Remond Henderson has been nominated.

Mr. Thomas Walton: On third and final call are there any further nominations for the office of Chairman of the National Board of Directors of Blacks In Government.

(No response)

Seeing no hands, we declare that the nominations are closed on the names of Mr. Farrell Chiles and Mr. Remond Henderson for the office of Chair of the National Board of Directors of Blacks In Government.

Mr. Thomas Walton: At this time, the Chair will recognize – according to Robert's, the last shall be first, the first shall be last. In this particular case, the Chair recognizes Mr. Remond Henderson for his platform.

Mr. Remond Henderson: Thank you, Mr. Chairman. Ladies and gentlemen of the Board of Directors, I stand here asking for your support in being the facilitator and a team leader for this organization. You were elected as Regional Directors and you were elected as leaders. All I want to do is help facilitate that leadership. You know why you wanted to be selected as a Regional Directors. Some of you are serving your first term, others not your first term. Those of you that are not serving your first term know what some of the problems are that we have had as a board that have not been corrected, that are not new problems. They just haven't been addressed. And we have the tools to address them. Those of you that are new, knowing how the grapevine works, you probably know just as much as those of us who have been around a long time.

What I propose to do is to hold people accountable. We have policies and procedures already in place. A lot of the thinking, a lot of hard dedicated work has gone into developing those policies and procedures. The problem is that we don't enforce our own policies and procedures that we've adopted. We don't enforce them because we don't hold people accountable. I intend, as Chair, to hold people accountable. I intend to be involved, not just to be an ad hoc member of the committees, I want to be actively in those committees and provide guidance.

I think that I've got the experience to provide that guidance in a couple of areas and not the experience in other areas. But in matters of finance and in matters of personnel, 30 years of experience in the financial arena; and, on top of that, being the National Treasurer for five years, believe me, I know about the finances of this organization.

I also have insights into how the office staff operates and the internal operations of the organization because I had almost daily contact with members of the National Office on a daily basis. What I would like to do is I think we need to reduce our administrative costs, and I think we need to allocate more costs to programs. And we can reduce administrative costs. Believe me, we can reduce administrative costs.

We can reduce administrative costs, specifically in the area of the conference. We waste a lot of money in the conference, and it would not take away anything from the conference itself, but we can reduce some expenditure.

I think we've got to increase our dollars in the program area because we are not going to increase the membership in this organization until we start providing something to the membership. And you can't provide things to membership without dollars, with the exception of one thing. The one thing that we should be providing to the membership is membership cards, and that is not rocket science. Somehow we can't seem to do that.

Well, I think that we should have a committee on the board to look into what it's going to take to get those membership cards out, at a minimum. I think that we could raise the visibility of the National Board of Directors, as far as I can see, has no visibility. Blacks In Government as an organization has very little visibility because the average person on the street does not know who Blacks In Government is. So as the Board of Directors, they definitely don't know who you are.

I think that the board can actively get involved with increasing corporate sponsors. The Executive Committee can do that. The Board of Directors can do that. It can be a concerted effort, a joint effort; but it doesn't mean that we have to leave it up to the Executive Committee just to go out and get corporate sponsorship. We can do that.

I ask you not to let politics get in the way of what you think is the most qualified person for this position I ask to be able to serve in this position for one year. If you don't like it, then elect someone next year. That simple.

If you think – if I'm elected and you think that I'm doing something wrong, then tell me. Pull me aside, call a recess. If you think I'm out of order, you think I've done something wrong, I'll listen. I am a team player. Regardless of what anyone says, I am a team player.

I would like to see this board not have any hidden agendas. And I would liked to see this board, when we go into executive session and we discuss things, and we leave and open the doors, that things that we discuss in executive session stay in executive session.

Ladies and gentlemen, I solicit your support. And thank you.

(Applause)

Mr. Thomas Walton: Thank you, Mr. Henderson. At this time the Chair recognizes Mr. Farrell Chiles.

Mr. Farrell Chiles: Thank you. First of all, I want to thank each of you for your support in 2003, and I want to request and solicit and ask for your vote for 2004 as the Chair of the National Board of Blacks In Government.

You know, the word is leadership, and that's what we all are. We're leaders. And this body is the leadership forum for this organization. And I believe that you lead by example. And I believe in results. And I want to take you back to the Year 2002 and bring you forward to 2004, just in terms of board management and administration.

If you look at the numbers, we spend less time in board meetings and that result in fewer pages of transcripts, less time that we have to pay for a transcriber to transcribe our business. That's business efficiency. We still get the business of the organization accomplished. So, I am very cost mindful of the organization and how we do business.

We don't have to conduct business until 12:00 at night anymore. We can do it during normal business hours and still be very effective.

In the area of membership, I believe that we need to provide more services to our members because that's the foundation of the organization; but also, the foundation of the organization is members, and I don't think there is anyone in this organization that has led the challenge to get more members in the organization, more life members in the organization, more gold plus members in the organization than myself.

Another area of cost savings is that I have agency support. I can go to two or three places and conduct the business of Blacks In Government at no cost to the organization. I just got back from a trip to Washington, D.C, that my agency supported; but because of their support, I was able to go to the National Executive Committee meeting and conduct some other business for the organization and raise additional funds for the organization.

We talk about corporate sponsorship and partnerships and membership. And we talk about CDC (Center for Disease Control) being the only corporate member that we gave and they are grand-fathered because they have been with us so long. Well, I've gone out and I've gotten a corporate member. It's a bronze member. So we have one more besides CDC. And I'm talking to other organizations. It's my commitment and my goal this year to bring in five corporate members. I have a list of names and I'm working with them diligently.

Last year during NTC, I brought in funds, corporate sponsorship for the luncheon. So that wasn't just financed by people attending the luncheon. We were supported by a corporation that sponsored us. They didn't just bring the money to you. You have to go out and you have to ask for it. So I have exhibited leadership in that area.

What I am saying is we have proven leadership. You have someone that's out there doing things for the organization. I don't do it in such a manner that I get a lot of attention, but I do it in such a way that we're effective and we're moving the organization forward.

I really believe that the membership sees this board in an entirely more positive light that it has over the years. So what I'm asking you to do today is to, again, vote for me as Chair of the Board. Provide the support we need to move the organization forward.

I am always open to communication. I talk to people on a weekly and a daily basis. I solicit your interests, your ideas, and input. But you know, we're all in this together, and it's not just one person that make the Board; it's the board collectively that determines the direction that we're going. And I believe we're going in a positive direction. I don't want to see us go backwards. And I really believe that I can best continue to move the organization and the board forward. So again, I ask for your vote and your support in 2004. Thank you.

(Applause)

Mr. Thomas Walton: Thank you, Mr. Chiles. In accordance with the motion that was previously passed, we have complied with Part A, and we have allowed the platforms of the two candidates who were nominated. The floor is now open for questions during the question and answer period to each of the candidates. Ms. Hampton.

Ms. David Hampton: I would like to ask the candidates if they have a communication plan that would facilitate the board being informed and staying updated with actions that are taking place in the National Office. And what would it be?

Mr. Farrell Chiles: A plan, per se, the answer is no; but I believe in communication. And I talk to the president. He is the person responsible for the day-to-day operations of the office staff and all those administrative functions that go on. And we talk a couple of times a week, either through e-mails, through messages. And when there is a concern, I express that concern. And if you notice, a lot of times I've sent him questions and I've sent them by e-mail and I've gotten the responses back so that everyone knows what's going on.

So do I have a plan? The answer is no. But as a board, we need to ensure that we're communicating with each other, and when something comes up that needs board attention, that we need to provide to the president, we need to do so. I don't go directly to the staff. I do everything through the president.

Mr. Remond Henderson: One, I too agree that there should be discussion and communication with the president, but I also believe that we have a Personnel Committee, and I think that the Personnel

Committee, obviously -- for some reason the daily communication or weekly communication or whatever it has been has not resolved some of the problems that we still have. And granted, some problems have been resolved, but there are others that still need to be resolved.

So I think that through the Personnel Committee, that would be the vehicle for addressing issues that are personnel related. And that's what I would liked to see done, is to work directly with the Personnel Committee and outline some procedures in accordance with our policies that – of what actions should be taken.

Dr. Doris Sartor: As you know, one of Blacks In Government's challenges is our financial situation. And, this is directed toward both candidates. What are some of the initiatives or ideas concerning generating revenue or cost savings other than corporate sponsorship, which has already been noted, and cutting off line item spending, that has already been noted" What I'm asking for are initiatives or ideas about generating revenue for the organization or cost savings ideas. And please be as specific as possible on those items.

Mr. Farrell Chiles: When you start talking about generating revenue, and we've talked about the corporate donations, corporate memberships, corporate sponsorships, that's one area that we're lacking in that can bring in additional revenue is in membership. We do not do a very good job of soliciting local and state and federal employees to join this organization. If we increased it by just 10,000 people at $35, that's additional revenue that can help us move forward as an organization.

I was at a conference in D.C. last week, and I went through the exhibition area; and one of the booths was run by an organization that publishes the Air Force Times, Navy Times and the Federal Times. And I got into a discussion with the lady and she is willing, for every subscription of Federal Times that Blacks In Government members take on, to provide rebates of $5. And over the years, you start accumulating, let's say, five years, and you get 5,000 people over a five year period, that's a significant amount of money.

The other portion of it is that we don't take advantage of grant writing because grants can provide additional revenue and provide the resources in terms of personnel to conduct programs. And what's so unfortunate is that we work for federal agencies and we have expertise among our members in federal agencies that provide grants. Well, in a lot of cases, review those grants and yet we don' take the initiative to do grants for Blacks In Government. So those are other opportunities for revenue.

Mr. Remond Henderson: First of all, we have to be very careful about what we do in terms of solicitation of revenue because we have to make sure that we're in compliance with our 510(c)(3) requirements, number one. And aside from that, taking that into consideration, then do I have a specific plan? Yes. When you say corporate sponsor, corporate sponsors doesn't necessarily always mean that it is an outright donation of dollars. There are services that can be donated that can cover costs. Some of the things, besides services – for example, I attended the National Association of Black Accountants Conference. Their portfolio was completely sponsored and paid for by a corporation. Now, it's an outright donation of corporate dollars, but we don't have to – the organization did not have to pay for those portfolios.

Those are the kinds of things that we can look at. Instead of outright dollars, there may be businesses that it would cost them very little to provide the things that we need that would cost a lot for us to spend the money on.

And grant writing. I agree that's something we can do. We did that in Region X and obtained some grants.

Mr. Remond Henderson: One other thing on that, I'm sorry. There is something else that we didn't do, and we have to look at this and whether or not we can do this, and that is rather or not we can have raffles. Raffles bring in money. You get things donated from businesses and raffle those things out. That's another way of generating funds.

Ms. Regina Kennedy: Question. The local, municipal and state government employees have expressed dissatisfaction with the focus of BIG being for the federal sector. What do you propose to do –or that would change that perception in order for us to do more with recruiting local, municipal and state employee chapters?

Mr. Remond Henderson: First of all, I think that the Executive Committee has appointed -- I think it's the responsibility of, I believe, the Second Vice-President who is a member – that's very dear to my heart, because I'm a state employee.

And many times when Blacks In Government is speaking, a lot of times there is no reference to state employees. A lot of times it's federal.

And I have been, as a Regional Council President for Region X, constantly making an emphasis in anything that we discuss, saying that we represent all levels of government.

In fact, in Region X we have – most of the individuals in Blacks In Government are members of city government and state government. Very few [are] federal employees.

But there is a committee that is already established or an individual. And, in fact, I think there is even a forum at the conference that we have to increase the membership and discuss state and local. But state and local, as well as federal, it's real difficult for us to go out and increase membership of this organization if we haven't gotten something to offer those members…The training conference is an excellent conference but members are looking for more than that.

And if you're going to go out and solicit more members, you have to have something to offer them and you have to have some programs; and I think that we need to look at some additional programs.

Mr. Farrell Chiles: It's very important that you answer the question, what's in it for me, because that's what they ask for; why should I join Blacks In Government? Fortunately, in the L.A. area, we get strong support and strong involvement from county and city public servants because we have programs that benefit them. And that's the bottom line. People will join when there is something in it for them. So what we have to do is come up with a program on the national level than can have the same effect that's in Seattle and in L.A. We also have to address their needs and concerns at the National Training Conference.

But you have to go to the local communities and find out what it is and what button to push to get people to join. And one of the successes that we have is that I have county people recruiting county people, state people recruiting state people, and city folks recruiting city folks, because they talk the language and they can sell why they joined much better than someone like me – but, you know, I can sell anything. You know, I used to be a used car salesman – but the key is you have to be able to reduce the space between the organization and those local and state workers in order for them to see that there is a benefit. If there is no benefit, there is no reason for them to join.

Ms. Katherine Cage: My question is since the Board Chair is elected annually, what is your short-term vision for the organization?

Mr. Farrell Chiles: My short-term vision is to move the organization continually forward. And when I say that, I mean that we need to have a very successful National Training Conference, we need to increase membership, we need to really market our gold plus program, and we need to come up with new benefits for our members to attract them and to continually get them to support our organization.

Mr. Remond Henderson: My short-term vision, I guess, would continue – I didn't run for Chair of the Board last year. I did run for Chair of the Board two years ago, and one of the things that I emphasized was that – is that we needed to conduct business more efficiently and get out on time. And so I can't say that I can improve that because I think Mr. Chiles has done a good job at that and I'm glad he followed my recommendation.

Mr. Farrell Chiles: You're welcome.

Mr. Remond Henderson: So in terms of short-term vision, I would just say, one, I would like to continue with timely meetings; but also, short-term vision – my short term-vision, as well as a successful conference is I think that we have committees established that are not completely functioning properly. I would like to see those committees functioning as they were designed to do.

And I would like to us following – and I won't be specific about this, but we have prescribed policies and procedures that we are not adhering to and we've taken some motions and taken action to have some motions that were passed that have not been followed up on and we've neglected.

My short-term vision is to go back and look at those things, with the input of board members, of things that we are – I don't think we need to go back and re-invent the wheel on some things, but we have some things that we have not completed. And that would be my short-term vision, to go back and identify those things.

Mr. Thomas Walton: Has everyone completed their ballots?

Mr. Thomas Walton: Ms. Cashwell and Ms. Samuel, what is the total number of ballots that you have collected?

Ms. Norma Samuel: 22.

Mr. Thomas Walton: One will read and the other will verify, please, the name that is on the ballot. And say it out loud.

Ms. Claire Cashwell: Farrell Chiles.

Ms. Norma Samuel: Farrell Chiles.

Ms. Claire Cashwell: Farrell Chiles.

Ms. Norma Samuel: Farrell Chiles.

Ms. Claire Cashwell: Remond Henderson.

Ms. Norma Samuel: Remond Henderson.

Ms. Claire Cashwell: Farrell Chiles.

Ms. Norma Samuel: Remond Henderson.

Ms. Claire Cashwell: Farrell Chiles.

Ms. Norma Samuel: Farrell Chiles.

Ms. Claire Cashwell: Farrell Chiles.

Ms. Norma Samuel: Farrell Chiles.

Ms. Claire Cashwell: Farrell Chiles.

Ms. Norma Samuel: Farrell Chiles.

Ms. Claire Cashwell: Farrell Chiles.

Ms. Norma Samuel: Farrell Chiles.

Ms. Claire Cashwell: Remond Henderson.

Ms. Norma Samuel: Remond Henderson.

Ms. Claire Cashwell: Remond Henderson.

Ms. Norma Samuel: Farrell Chiles.

Ms. Claire Cashwell: Farrell Chiles.

Ms. Norma Samuel: Farrell Chiles.

Mr. Thomas Walton: The number of votes necessary for election -- the number of votes cast is 22. Necessary for election would be twelve. Mr. Farrell Chiles has 16 votes; Mr. Remond Henderson has 6. The Chair declares Mr. Farrell Chiles re-elected as Chair of the National Board of Directors.

(Applause)

The Board meeting was in San Diego - in Region IX. I drove the two hours from my home to the meeting. I was in my country. Several people from my chapter – the Los Angeles/Long Beach Area Chapter was in attendance at the beginning of the meeting, to include Chapter Charter members Charles Townsend and Everlena McGowan. Additionally, Earl Bryers, the former president of the Greater San Diego Chapter and the region's Second Vice-President, Horace Hill Jr., Greater San Diego Chapter President; and Bernard Smith, President of the Customs and Border and Protection Chapter. The Board received greetings from William Blair, Assistant to U.S. Congressman Bob Filner; Tony Young, representative of the City of San Diego; and John Reyes, Vice-President of Sales for the San Diego Convention and Visitors Bureau.

After the Chair and Vice Chair elections, the Board spent a considerable amount of time in Executive Session discussing the latest developments pertaining to the Arthur Henderson case and other legal issues.

During the course of the meeting, I made the following committee chair appointments: Awards – Richard Shields; Constitution and Policy, Constitution – Dr. Doris Sartor; Constitution and Policy, Policy – Ellen Dyson; Constitution and Policy, By-laws – Darlene Young; Financial Advisory and Oversight – Oscar Williams; Personnel – Katherine Cage; Program Oversight – Daniel Corria; Strategic Planning – David Hampton; Time and Place/Delegates Assembly – C. Jacquie Beatty.

After much discussion, I did not appoint a chair of the ad hoc Capital Fund-Raising Committee. We dissolved the committee. A motion was made to accept the appointments presented by the Chair. The motion passed. I then assigned members of the Board to the various committees.

The Board received the President's report; Treasurer's Report; an update on the 2004 National Training Conference; and a report from the National Delegates Assembly Chair (Mr. Thomas Walton).

The Board approved:

- A motion that the President prepare an aggressive operational plan outlining actions he will take to curtail deficit spending by standing committees and office staff and present the plan at the next Board meeting for approval.
- The by-laws of five chapters.
- The selection of Bert Smith and Company as our auditors and for the President to sign an engagement letter for the audit to begin by February 24, 2004 and a target date for completion of March 31, 2004.
- That the President provides comments to the audit management letter by February 15, 2004.
- The name change of the Policy Manual to the Policies and Procedures Manual.
- That the President provide the BIG membership feedback on BIG's efforts in addressing a revision in the new EEOC Management Directive -715 by 1 March 2004.
- A motion for the Executive Committee budget funding for Region IX's Officer Leadership Training or provide funding to the region's master trainers to implement training and fund the chapters' regional representatives as outlined in the scheduled OLT process that was postponed.
- The revision of several policies.
- The approval of two interest groups as BIG Chapters, and
- A motion that the President provide a template for a concise report of the National Training Conference, specifically the financial section inclusive of how much was spent on each line item (by March 1, 2004).

The meeting adjourned on Saturday evening, January 31st at 7:20 p.m. For fun, some Board members went to a local gambling casino. You can do those kinds of things when you adjourn at a decent time. They borrowed my car. I was hoping to get at least one future vote from my generous gesture. That's politics.

Board Meeting; April 2, 2004; Sheraton Suites; Houston, Texas

The meeting was called to order at 9:15 a.m. Mr. Thomas Walton led all assembled with an opening prayer. We acknowledged our guests and received greetings from Karl Hartfield, the Greater Houston Convention and Visitors Bureau; George R. Brown, Director of Sales of Reliant Park; Nina Jackson, Director of Marketing and Public Relations for Reliant Park; and Marcus Milburn, Group Sales Manager for the Sheraton Suites Houston. We conducted roll call, established a quorum, approved the agenda and went about the business of Blacks In Government.

We spent a considerable amount of time in Executive Session discussing and making decision on the Arthur Henderson Case and other legal matters.

We passed several motions.

Before we adjourned, C. Jacquie Beatty on behalf of the Board, thanked Region VI for their hospitality.

The meeting adjourned on Saturday evening, April 2, 2004 at 6:36 p.m. At the conclusion of the meeting we were transported by bus to the Houston Convention Center for a tour of the facility and a delicious dinner.

I had an early wake up call for the next morning to take a shuttle to the airport. The hotel failed to call my room and I missed my shuttle. However, all was not lost. They provided a courtesy sedan service for me and I still made my flight and at no cost to BIG.

Board Meeting; August 13, 2004; Marriott Wardman Park Hotel; Washington, D.C.

The meeting was called to order a 9:00 a.m. Roll call was conducted and the Cynthia Davis, the National Secretary, advised me that we did not have a quorum. So the Board took a ten minutes recess and reconvened at 9:15 a.m. Charles Oliver, Board Member, Region X, led us in our opening prayer. We established a quorum, approved the agenda, and went about conducted the business of Blacks In Government. After the minutes of the previous meeting were approved, the Regional Directors gave their reports.

The Board approved the by-laws revisions of several chapters; two chapter name changes; and approved the charters of the West Chicago United (Region VI), North Providian (Region III), the Eugene County Chapter (Region X), and the McNamara Chapter Defense Logistics Agency (Region XI).

On a motion by Dr. Doris Sartor, the Board directed the National President to publish BIG's position and strategies as related to the National Security Personnel System (NSPS) within sixty days.

The Constitution & Policy (Constitution) provided the Board with its recommendations to adopt or not to adopt eleven constitution amendment changes submitted by the membership (individual members, chapters, and regions). The Board accepted all but one of their recommendations.

During the meeting, Ms. Dorothy Page-Proctor of Bert Smith & Company (BIG's auditors) presented the Board with its 2003 audit and management letter. After the presentation and much discussion, Oscar Williams made a motion that we accept the financial statements of the auditor so that we could disseminate it to the Delegates Assembly. The motion passed.

At 2:15 p.m., we moved out of general session and went into Executive Session at 2:30 p.m. The first item in the Executive Session was to receive an update on our legal issues. Mr. Ronald Jessamy, our outside attorney, provided us with a summary and status of each case and answered Board members' questions. The Board discussed other issues, approved the minutes of the previous Executive Session, and came out of Executive Session at 4:30 p.m.

Once in General Session, the Financial Advisory/Oversight Committee gave a report on their review of BIG's accounting operations. The committee performed the review on two occasions – June 22nd through 24th and on July 16th and 17th. The committee made several recommendations to improve the internal procedures for maintaining a daily log to track receipt of mail and its final destination.

The committee identified other areas of non-compliance of several operating policies and made a series of motions for the president to ensure that the office staff complied with procedures as outlined in the personnel manual. At 6:52 p.m., the Board recessed.

On Saturday, August 14th, the Board reconvened at 9:00 a.m. After a quorum was established, Abe Joseph, the National Treasurer, gave the Treasurer's report. Mr. Joseph thanked Regions III, V, VII, and IX for 100% compliance. He then made a motion to revoke certain chapters' charters for not filing their financial reports for 2002. The motion carried. The Board took a break at 9:45 a.m. and reconvened at 10:32 a.m. and accepted committee reports. At 6:40 p.m., the Board recessed until Thursday, August 19th.

The Board reconvened at 2:00 p.m. on the 19th. A quorum was established and the Board commenced to finish its business. The Constitution and Policy Committee (Policy) made motions to revise several policies – Policy 1:27; Policy 1:32; and Policy 3:13. We established a new policy – Policy 1:33-A, and added another new policy titled – Management of Salaried Staff. The Board also approved the deletion of the proviso from Policy 2:08.

On Friday evening, five minutes after the Closing Plenary Session, the Board met briefly and officially adjourned.

Board Meeting; October 29, 2004; Double Tree Hotel; Kansas City, Missouri

The meeting was called order at 9:07 a.m. Mr. Thomas Walton led us in prayer. We had guests in attendance, so we went around the room and introduced ourselves. A quorum was established. We approved an amended agenda and the minutes of the previous meeting were approved with corrections. We then went about the business of Blacks In Government.

During the course of the meeting, the Board approved several actions, to include:

- Approval of New York City for NTC 2007; Nashville, Tennessee for 2008; and New Orleans, Louisiana for 3009.
- Approval of revisions to Policies 2:04 and 3:12.
- The Bylaw subcommittee's recommendations on new models for chapter bylaws and regional council bylaws.
- An additional conference fee of $25.00 to every NTC conference registrant to be divided equally to the Regions.
- The temporary hiring of the Accounts Payable Clerk position.
- Authorization of a 3 percent Cost of Living Adjustment (COLA) for all employees assigned to a permanent position, effective January 1, 2005.

Prior to adjourning the meeting, I thanked everyone for a very productive year. The Board adjourned at 11:55 p.m. on Saturday, October 30, 2004.

Chapter 8: Make it Four in a Row 2005

"The best leader is the one who has sense enough to pick good men to do what he wants done, and the self-restraint to keep from meddling with them while they do it." – Theodore Roosevelt

Blacks In Government
National Board of Directors Meeting
Embassy Suites Hotel
Washington, D.C.
Friday, January 28, 2005

Excerpts from the official transcript:

Mr. Farrell Chiles: Good morning. It is January 28, 2005. The National Board of Directors of Blacks In Government is officially called to order. The time is 8:16 a.m. I'd like to start the session off with an opening prayer. Mr. Walton, will you do us the honors, please?...

Mr. Farrell Chiles: Next item on the agenda, election of the Board Chair and Vice Chair. And at this point I will yield the floor to Mr. Walton.

Mr. Thomas Walton: Thank you Mr. Chair. In accordance with the National Constitution of Blacks In Government, Article VI, the duties of the National Elected Officers and Appointed Positions, Committees and Staff, Section 1: Section 1-B: The Chair of the Board of Directors serve as Chair of the Board of Directors, officially transmits the policies which have been approved by the Board of Directors, recommends to the Board of Directors changes in policies and procedures, presents the organization's annual report to the annual Delegates Assembly, appoints committee chairs of the board with the consent of the board, and is an ex-officio member of the board committees; requires reports on the activities of the Regional Councils and the chapters -- through the Board of Directors from the regions and board committees; performs such functions and exercises such other authority as may be prescribed by the Board of Directors. The Chair of the board cannot be a member of the Executive Committee...

From the Board Policy 3:07, Subject, Election of the Board Chair: "The election of the Board Chair, the election of the Chair and Vice Chair of the Board of Directors shall be by secret ballot, with the majority vote for the election unless there is but one nomination for the Chair or Vice Chair, in which case the election shall be by acclamation.

If there is not one elected on the first ballot, then the two candidates with the highest number of votes for the Chair or Vice Chair will participate in a run-off election for their respective position.

Nominations shall be from the floor. The term of the office for the Chair and Vice Chair shall be for one year or until their successors are elected. The term of office shall begin immediately following the election. The effective date [is] 9 January 1993, Board of Directors meeting"...

Mr. Thomas Walton: The floor is now open for nominations for Chair of the Board of Directors of Blacks In Government.

Mr. Charles Oliver: Charles Oliver, Region X. I want to nominate Mr. Remond Henderson.

Mr. Thomas Walton: Mr. Remond Henderson has been nominated. Any further nominations for the office of Chair of the National Board of Directors?

Dr. Doris Sartor: Doris Sartor, Region IV. Mr. Farrell Chiles.

Mr. Thomas Walton: Mr. Farrell Chiles has been nominated. Are there any further nominations for the office of Chair of the National Boards of Directors of Blacks In Government?

Mr. Gerald Reed: Gerald Reed, BIG Pentagon, Region XI. I nominate J. David Reeves.

Mr. Thomas Walton: Mr. J. David Reeves has been nominated...

Mr. Thomas Walton: Seeing no hands and hearing no voices, the nominations are closed on the names of Mr. Remond Henderson, Mr. Farrell Chiles, [and] Mr. J. David Reeves...

Mr. Thomas Walton: As we did last year, and we wanted to repeat again this year, to give the Board members an opportunity to ask question of the candidates. Last night, you were given cards to be passed out where you could actually write out questions that were to be present to me. So we're going to give all three candidates an opportunity to respond. Gentlemen, we would ask that you do not -- in the interest of time and that we have another appointment; that we try to give you at least three minutes, if you need to take that much time.

The question is – this is to all three candidates – "Do you have the fortitude to stand behind proper but controversial decisions?"

Mr. J. David Reeves: Good morning, Board members. I think my experience in Blacks In Government and your knowing me, knows that I have never been a person who did not take a stand. I believe in the best of Blacks In Government, and, even when I stand alone, have often voted in positions that I thought was in the best interest of Blacks In Government, even if I stood alone. I have never been one to shy away from tough decisions. I am a decision maker. I am not one to move in a direction in which I have to waffle or be wishy-washy in anything that I do. I think my more than fifteen years of experience in this organization demonstrates that.

I think that it is time that the leadership, particularly now as we move into, in some ways, a financial crisis situation in this organization, as we face some of the issues in terms of lawsuits, as we move in a direction in which the organization shows some possibility of conflict, that you need a leader that is willing to face the music and do it to a strong hand, as well as with a gentle heart. I think I am that candidate. I think I have demonstrated that I have leadership ability.

I never thought this organization or any organization intended to have any particular person in lead for any significant period of time. In the history of this organization we have never had a Board Chair that exceeded more than three years consecutively in this organization. There is a reason for that.

The organization is designed so that many people would have an opportunity to show their hand at leadership. I think that I can do that. I think my history presents that, and I think there is no doubt that I am the kind of person who can lead this organization, along with our newly elected president, in a way that we can work harmoniously together.

I'm sure you understand that Ms. Young and I have a wonderful working relationship, and I think that I can make the kind of decisions that you will be pleased with. Thank you.

Mr. Remond Henderson: I guess I would just echo what Mr. Reeves just said. If there is one controversial item what has always been on the agenda at this table has been the finances, and all of you can attest that I've always held my ground on that, regardless of how controversial it is; and that I've always stood for what I think is the best interest of the organization and have always had the financial concerns of the organization at heart.

And I think that particularly this year and maybe not in 2006 but in 2005, that is probably the most important thing that this organization needs to pay attention to; and I think that I am the most qualified candidate to lead you through this particular year, given those circumstances. Given the financial status, given the lawsuits that we have, I think that my background would best suit the organization at this point in time.

Mr. Farrell Chiles: The answer to the question is yes. I believe I have the fortitude. I believe that I have shown that I have the fortitude over the last three years as Board Chair, and I will continue to not only serve as Chair and reflect the decisions of the whole body as we go forth.

We have some challenging issues before us, and collectively we have to make the decisions together – based on everything that we all bring to the table; and keeping that in mind, I've worked with everyone over the last three years as the Board Chair, and prior to that as a Board member.

So my record is well-established that I care about the organization. I care about making the right decisions, and I care about executing those decisions that the Board make, and I will continue to do that. Thank you.

Mr. Thomas Walton: Thank you, gentlemen. The second question, "Will you place politics, in parenthesis, debts to supporters, above the good of Blacks In Government or vice versa?"

Mr. Remond Henderson: I'll go first this time. I'm not quite sure I understand the question, but I will say this: As far as I'm concerned, politics of the consideration is at the lowest level; that the organization should come first and politics should come last. And I think that in many times we make too many decisions based on politics.

Mr. J. David Reeves: I'll go next. I haven't had a discussion with any person in this room intentionally. I have made no commitments. I have made no promises. I have not called you and said, if you vote for me, then I will give you this position, you will have this, because while I am quite pleased, I think, with the leadership and the persons who sit in any of the positions; and if I was elected, would probably make very few changes in chairs of committees, I think it's important that you not play the politics.

That's our problem now. This organization is too dag-on political. We have forgotten the mission of this organization. We spend entirely too much time trying to get this vote and get that vote, and it's really more important of what is the need of the people who we were elected to serve. And we spend so much time around this table playing politics. I think that too often we forget that we are not here for that. We are here to serve the interest of our members.

Again, you know me. I'm straightforward, straight from the hip. I give you what I believe is in my heart and what is in the best interest of those persons that I was elected by and who I serve and the interest of this organization. I love this organization. There is no question, I think, about that; and I think that you can recognize that I'm the kind of person who can put politics aside and to the business that were elected to do.

Mr. Farrell Chiles: I agree with both of my opponents. The most important thing is making the best decisions for the organization. When it comes down to the bottom line, that's what we're here for, to set the policies and guide this organization so that we can continue to move forward. And that's my pledge to you that I will continue to do that and work with the Board to make sure that we make the right decisions for the national organization.

Mr. Thomas Walton: Thank you, gentlemen. The third and final question that I've received, "How do you propose to positively impact the Board's performance? In my opinion, the Board performs mediocrity. How do you propose to positively impact the Board's performance? In my opinion, the Board performs mediocrity."

Mr. J. David Reeves: I propose that what we need to do is that we need to develop a more – a better form of communication. We spend so much time, again, playing politics; that we fail to recognize the importance of what the issues are; and I think oftentimes it's because there is lack of communication.

As Board members, we come into the room oftentimes, and we don't know what decisions that may have been made by the Board Chair in the interim of the meeting. We don't know what kind of papers have come in because oftentimes they don't even appear on the web site. And so we are forced to have to deal with issues at the spare of the moment. I think every piece of paper that comes in that affects the Board's decision need to be discussed. There are ways that you can communicate before the Board meeting. There are e-mail issues. There are conference calls. There are ways that we ought to collectively work together as a family.

I think too often that is not what we have done. We have not been a family. We have not been a team. We have been individuals of one or two in regions who walk in and just say this is how we feel. We, it ought to be before we even get to the room on Thursday or Friday night that we've already had the discussion electronically, or we've had the discussion in ways that will help enhance the organization.

And while we may not be making decisions, we certainly ought to know what is in the best interest of this organization. So they are to improve communication, to ensure that everyone is on the same page and that everyone has the same understanding. And while we may not always agree, we certainly can reach the same conclusions based upon what is in the best interest of this organization.

Mr. Farrell Chiles: We need to do a better job at communicating, but, you know, communicating is a 25 people process. We all have to share in the communication, and so often we hoard what we have until we want to bring it out and a lot of times that's at an inappropriate time. What I've always wanted folks to do is even with Regional Council reports or your Regional Directors' reports - you share it immediately with us. We don't wait until we do the pass-around. Share the information because from that something may come to light that someone else can bring attention to, to help us through the process.

When we have the Thursday round table discussions, that's another time where we build on that communication so that we don't bring hidden agendas and surprises to the Board meeting, so we're all on the same sheet of music.

So it takes all of us working together and communicating and being open and honest with each other. And my goal, again, is to try to bridge the gap between non-communications to the communication so that we can work together effectively as a team to make the right decisions for the Board and for the National organization.

Mr. Remond Henderson: First of all, in terms of committees. I would not make any change on Chairs of committees unless there were some strains or challenges or objections to the Committee Chairs that exist right now, with the exception of one committee, and I will talk about that in just a second.

But in terms of our Board, I think that we need to cut down on the discussion on various topics when we hear the same thing repeated over and over again by different Board members, regurgitation of the same thing over and over again when we've already heard a position and someone has stated the same position.

I think that we need to have transcripts available so that we don't have to go back and try to figure out, in addition to the minutes, what was stated in the last meeting and what the intent of the motion was. If we have that transcript available and don't have to go back and research it through the computer, we need to have it hard copy sitting right there at the table.

And finally, finally, I think that one of the most important ways that this Board can function is that we have to give a strong emphasis on the Finance Committee because the Finance Committee should be involved with all of the other operational committees, just like a corporation and just like an entity. The center and the focus of anything are finances. Anything builds on that. And what I see that we need to do is we need to have the Finance Committee, this committee right here, has oversight of the Treasurer, all other committees – the Treasurer, committees, and the National President and the Executive Committee.

There needs to be relationship – and you talked about communication – between all of these things, but the center point and the focal point is the Finance Committee. And I think that if we develop that relationship that everyone understands, that the Finance Committee is the focal point, that it will improve the operations and cut down on a lot of discussions.

We spend so much time at every meeting talking about the Treasurer's report and the finances. We spend more time on that than any other subject, and I think that if we can formalize how we – how the Treasurer and the Finance Committee operate, that will make the Board more efficient in the long run.

Mr. Thomas Walton: Board members, I have one final question. Without objection, I would like for you to consider it, please. I believe it's in the best interest of the organization. It says, "How do you plan to enforce compliance with Board directive?" How do you plan to enforce compliance with Board directive?"

Mr. Remond Henderson: Well, there is a long-standing battle that the Board is responsible for development of policies and procedures, compliance issues, and the Executive Committee is responsible for – I just wanted to make sure that I had your attention. A slight interruption there -- for -- responsible for compliance.

The bottom line is we have to hold people accountable, and the problem is we don't hold people accountable. There are no sanctions whatsoever when someone is not in compliance. At most we slap somebody's hand and ignore it, and politics take over.

And we've got to put politics aside, and the only way that you can do that is to hold people accountable on the record. And you start holding people accountable for their actions or inactions. That's how you make the change.

Mr. Chiles: Again, there is nothing to disagree on. The key is holding people accountable. But what does that mean? That means that the Board has to do an action, and once you do that action, the Board has to enforce the action. Slapping people on the wrist is one thing, but you have to do something stronger if you want to make a statement, and that takes a Board action.

So the Board has to stand up and make the right decision and enforce it. And until we do that, it's just a slap on the wrist. So it's us, working together, knowing that we need to do the right thing and following through on it.

Mr. J. David Reeves: I believe that it's important that we do take sanctions against Board members who – or members or Executive Committee members or whoever is a part of this organization that is causing conflict. I think that begins with the leadership.

If you have weak leadership, you get weak results. If you have people who are not willing to enforce the hard decisions, then you get weak decisions. I think the leadership has to demonstrate and present to the body oftentimes the tough things to do. Nobody said that when you were elected Board Chair, that it was going to be an easy job. I don't anticipate the job as being easy. I've sat on this Board for four years. I know we have tough decisions.

But, it's important that as the Chair, that that person takes the bull by the horns and then makes the decision that this is a direction that is in the best interest of Blacks In Government and takes a firm stand to lead the organization, to lead the Board members and to explain the consequences of our actions or our inactions.

I think it's very critical that at this juncture, that we begin to recognize that we have to stop playing with this thing. This organization is going down the tubes if we don't get it together. And I think we all know that. It's time for us to quit playing Board members. It's time for us to be Board members and to be strong in our decisions, our commitments, and make the tough decisions when the tough decisions need to be made.

Mr. Thomas Walton: That concludes our question and answer period…Without objection; we will proceed then to the election process…

The teller, Ms. Faye Stewart-Henderson, the National Assistant Treasurer, informed me that we have 25 ballots. She will now read those ballots, and Ms. Lee will record them.

Ms. Stewart-Henderson: All right.

Farrell Chiles.
Remond Henderson.
Farrell Chiles.
J. David Reeves.
Remond Henderson.
Farrell Chiles.
Farrell Chiles.
Farrell Chiles.
Farrell Chiles.
J. David Reeves.
Farrell Chiles.
Farrell Chiles.
Farrell Chiles.
Farrell Chiles.
Farrell Chiles.
Farrell Chiles.
Remond Henderson.
Remond Henderson.
Remond Henderson.
Farrell Chiles.
J. David Reeves.
Farrell Chiles.
J. David Reeves.
Remond Henderson.
Farrell Chiles.

Mr. Thomas Walton: Farrell Chiles has received 15 votes. Mr. Remond Henderson has received 6 votes. Mr. J. David Reeves [received] 4 votes. We declare Mr. Farrell Chiles re-elected as the Chair of the National Board of Directors of Blacks In Government.

At the beginning of the meeting and after the agenda had been approved, the first item on the agenda was the Chairman's appointment of two new board members. My policy was for the Regional Council president to send me a letter recommending the appointment of the individual, minutes from the Regional Council meeting verifying the vote for the individual, and a bio of the recommended person. Region VIII recommended John Lyons, a former Board Vice-Chair, to fill the unexpired term of Richard Shields, who was elected as the National Third Vice-President. Region XI recommended Gerald Reed, former National President, to fill the unexpired term of Darlene Young, the incoming National President. Both appointments were approved by the Board.

The Board recessed at 9:28 am to attend the installation of officers' ceremony at the Department of State headquarters in the Dean Acheson Auditorium. We boarded vans at 9:45 a.m. and proceeded to the 23rd Street entrance. After going through security, we were escorted to a holding room prior to the start of the ceremony.

While we were in the holding room, in another part of the building, Condoleezza Rice was being sworn in as the new Secretary of State, the first African-American female to hold the position. After her swearing in by Vice-President Dick Cheney, the Secretary came by the holding room, greeted us, spoke briefly, took time for some photo-ops, and then departed.

During the installation ceremony, I introduced the Board to the attendees and gave a speech on the Board's composition and members' profile. The Board was sworn in, then the Executive Committee, followed by the National President. After the ceremony, there was a reception in another area of the building.

The Board reconvened at 3:16 p.m. and we proceeded to conduct the business of the organization. We approved the minutes of the previous meeting and received the President's and Treasurer's reports.

Prior to recessing for committee meetings, I made my committee chairs appointments: Johnita Pitts – Awards; J. David Reeves – Constitution and Policy, Constitution; Ellen Dyson – Constitution and Policy, Policy; Delores Ivy – Constitution and Policy, By-laws; Oscar Williams – Financial Advisory/Oversight; Katherine Cage – Personnel; Doris Sartor – Program Oversight; David Hampton –

Strategic Planning; C. Jacquie Beatty – Time & Place /Delegates Assembly.

J. David Reeves moved for the acceptance of the committee chairs as presented by the Board Chair. Alma Garlington seconded the motion. The motion was approved without objection. I then made the rest of the committee assignments.

Some of the action items/motions approved by the Board during the January meeting:

- Suspension of non-compliant chapters with less than ten members.
- Suspension of chapters for non-compliance of Calendar Year 2003 financial reporting requirements.
- Approval of the President's appointments of the Standing Committee Chairs.
- Approval of five chapters' by-laws.
- Approval of two interest groups' charters.
- Accepted the FA&OC's recommendation to move $100,000 from the Merrill Lynch investment account and $77,000 from the net proceeds of the 1820 National Office to the general operating account.
- Passed a motion that we make a public statement that BIG believes that the situation in the Sudan should be resolved immediately.
- Approved an on-the-spot cash award for a BIG staff member.
- Approved the revision of the Personnel Manual, Section 12, entitled, "Disciplinary Procedures".
- Agreed to hold the April 2006 Board meeting in Cleveland, Ohio.

The Board adjourned at 11:21 p.m. on Saturday, January 30, 2005.

The next day, I made reservations for an early Sunday Brunch at a D.C. restaurant called Georgia Brown's and invited several people that did not have early morning departures to attend. It had snowed the prior night and continued into Sunday and it was difficult to get a taxi. But, for those of us that went to the brunch, we enjoyed the food (for me, especially the grits), had good conversation, and we were entertained by a wonderful jazz band. I had a 3:30 p.m. American Airlines flight back to Los Angeles and I had spent another productive weekend away from home.

Board Meeting; April 15, 2005; Homewood Suites Hotel; Columbia, South Carolina

The meeting was called to order at 9:12 am. We were led in an opening prayer by Charles Oliver, Region X. Alice Mercer, the Immediate Past President, Region IV and Vickie Wheeler, Executive Vice-President of the East Central Savannah River Area Chapter gave greetings. After roll call, the approval of the agenda and the minutes of the January 2005 meeting, the Board went into Executive Session from 9:59 a.m. to 11:13 a.m. to review and discuss legal matters.

After returning to the general session, the Board received the President's report. Action items included motions to grant the National Treasurer and the National President the authority to sign the 2007 NTC Nashville and 2008 New Orleans contracts (which were over $25,000) once the hotels had concurred with BIG's changes. The motions passed. The Board approved the extensions of the Accountant position and the contract for the Accounts Payable position until August 31, 2005. The Board approved the appointment of Ida Tyree-Hyche as the Chair for the Legal Review Committee. We accepted the resignation of the Chair of the Legislative and Review Committee and approved the appointment of Glenn Smith, Region III, for the position. Other action items were referred to appropriate Board Committees for review and consideration.

The Board was provided status reports on the 2005 NTC by Ms. Peggy Wilson and the 2006 NTC by Ms. Alma Garlington. Darlene Young gave the final 2004 NTC report.

At 2:05 p.m. we recessed until 9:00 a.m. the following morning for committee meetings.

On Saturday, April 16, 2005, we reconvened 9:17 a.m. We established a quorum and went about conducting the business of the organization. The National President completed her report and then we received the Treasurer's report. A motion was passed for all regions to receive their 2003 NTC money by July 1, 2005 and that the 2004 NTC money due to all regions are paid by October 1, 2005. An amendment was passed to the motion to include the $25,000 due to Region XI in 2004 (as the host region) be paid by October 1, 2005 based on the completion of the 2004 audit.

Other motions approved by the Board during the meeting included:

- Approval of the recipients of the BIG Prestige Awards – Ms. Beverly Lyn-Cook and Ms. Barbara Johnson Cox for the Meritorious Service Award. The BIG Greater Kansas City, Inc. Chapter and the NOAA Chapter for the Distinguished Service Award, and Ms. Nita M. Jones of AARP-California for the Special Achievement Award.
- Approved the revised by-laws of four chapters.
- Approved revision of Policy 3:17 and the deletion of Policy 3:11.
- Approved the FA/OC recommended responses to the FY 2003 Management Letter.
- Approved the contract with the vendor for the NTC 2005 audio/video services not to exceed $65,000.
- Approved the recommendation that the January 2006 Board meeting be held in Richmond, Virginia.
- Approval to develop a support system for members whose jobs have been outsourced through government A76 studies.
- Granted a chapter charter to the Greater Bay Area Chapter (Region IX).

The Board meeting adjourned at 6:05 p.m., Saturday April 16, 2005. We had conducted the business of the organization and had the rest of the evening off.

Board Meeting; July 29, 2005; Peabody Hotel; Orlando, Florida

The meeting was called to order at 9:23 a.m. Charles Oliver led us with an opening prayer. We received greeting from Region Four (Ms. C. Jacquie Beatty). A quorum was established and the revised agenda was approved. The minutes were approved as corrected and we went about the business of Blacks In Government. In preparation for the Delegates Assembly scheduled for the upcoming Sunday, the Board approved the chartering of two interest groups; the Tuscaloosa Metro (Region IV) and the Department of Interior (Region XI). The Board removed several chapters from the suspension list; a couple of chapters from the revocation list; and approved two chapter name changes – the Department of Housing and Urban Development Chapter to the Robert C. Weaver Chapter (Region XI) and the BIG @ Fort Meade Chapter to the BIG @ IMA Chapter.

The Board considered the recommendations of the Constitution and Policy Committee's (Constitution Committee) on amendments submitted for Delegates Assembly action. The Board approved all thirteen of their recommendations to adopt or not to adopt.

At 11:52 a.m., the Board went into Executive Session for the purpose f receiving the audit report from our auditors firm, Bert & Company. Unfortunately, the auditors were unable to give us an opinion because some outstanding issues still unresolved. We did not receive a final report for the Delegates Assembly.

The Board discussed other BIG issues in Executive Session, approved previous Executive Session minutes and ended at 4:35 p.m.

Board Meeting; November 18, 2005; Doubletree Hotel; Little Rock, Arkansas

The meeting was called to order at 9:20 a.m. I asked Charles Oliver to lead us in prayer. Prior to the prayer, Mr. Oliver asked us to give a moment of silence for the Hurricane Katrina and Rita victims and for the Mother of the Civil Rights, Rosa Parks, who had just passed. Then we received greetings from Region VI, established a quorum, approved the amended agenda, and the minutes of the previous meeting.

The next item on the agenda was the President's report. Darlene Young presented several action items, all which were tabled, pending review by the appropriate Board committee.

The President moved that the Board accept the resignation of the Chair of the National Communications and Public Relations Committee. The motion was adopted without objection. The Board was then presented with reports on the NTC 2004, 2005, and 2006.

The Board temporarily suspended the President's report to receive the Auditor's report via teleconference. After the Auditor's report, the President resumed her report which was followed by the Treasurer's report before we recessed for committee meetings at 7:00 p.m.

The Board reconvened on Saturday morning at 9:28 a.m. After roll call and the establishing of a quorum, we went into Executive Session to discuss legal matters, personnel issues, and to approve previous Executive Session minutes. We stayed in Executive Session until 4:46 p.m.

Once the Board returned to general session, we considered and approved several motions. Some of the motions were:

- Approved the President's appointment of Felicia Shingler, Region XI, as the Chair of the National Communications and Public Relations Committee
- Approved Peggy Wilson, Region IV, as the Chair of Evaluations
- Approved for the Region IV Council to receive $25,000 (a percentage of the total net conference revenue in accordance with Board policy 1:27)
- Approved the City of Baltimore, Maryland for NTC 2009 and Kansas City, Missouri for NTC 2010
- Approved the revised by-laws of four chapters
- Approved the revisions of policies 2:10, 3:20, 1:14, 1:12, 3:21, 3:22, 1:00, 1:01, 1:20, 2:01, 2:08 and the approval of policy 1:42

- Approved to increase the NTC registration fee by $50.00 for members and non-members
- Approved the FA/OC FY 2006 budget recommendations
- Approved the final draft of the financial statement ending December 31, 2004.
- Approved revisions of the STACK guidelines
- Approved that the National Student award winners receive monetary awards as opposed to computers
- Approved the chartering of the Hardin County Metropolitan Area Interest Group, Fort Knox, Kentucky
- Revoked the charter of the Oakland (CA) Bay Area Chapter.

Before the Board adjourned, we went around the room for the Good of the Order. Some of the comments were:
Mr. Browne: It's been a good ride.
Mr. Dan Corria: I would like to say thanks to all the Board members.
Ms. Alma Garlington: It's been a pleasure working with the Board and I wish everyone good health and happiness.
Ms. Joyce Jones: I wish everybody a safe trip back home tomorrow.
Ms. Johnita Pitts: To all the Board members that are leaving, I wish you the best and enjoy.
Ms. Regina Kennedy: It's been a good long meeting.
Ms. Jacquie Beatty: I have enjoyed serving these last eight years on the Board. It's been a lot of work and I've taken some beatings, but I've enjoyed it.
Dr. Doris Sartor: I also have enjoyed serving on the Board. I've learned a lot, and I appreciate the friendship and the advice that I've received from those around the Board.
Ms. Ellen Dyson: I just want to say it's been real and welcome the new Board members. And for me, this will be the first time, come 31 December, it will be the first time in 23 years that I have not held a position in Blacks In Government; and I am looking forward to seeing if there is life after BIG.

Mr. Oscar Williams: I wish everyone a safe trip and enjoy their holidays, and I look forward to seeing everyone either at the Board meeting in January or at the NTC in New York.
Ms. Angela Thorpe-Harris: I thank the Little Rock Chapter for their hospitality. Good luck to our Board members who are coming back and safe travels.
Ms. Katherine Cage: I just want to say goodbye to the outgoing Board members. It's been a pleasure working with you. I have your phone numbers. I will call. I will e-mail, and I look forward to working with the new Board members; and safe travels home to everyone.
Ms. David Hampton: Well, to the Board members who are going off, it will be hard for me to come to Board meetings because I've never been here when you weren't here. So most of you were here ever since I've been on the Board, and I've enjoyed working with you. It is great having your friendship, learning to share with you. To the new Board members who are coming, I've worked with a number of you in other capacities, and it will be exciting to have you come on this Board and see what it's like to live through this process; and I welcome you and hope that we can become more effective and be into that strategic plan.
Ms. Delores Ivy: To the new Board members, welcome. And also, the road dog that I was referring to earlier, Julius is going to be proud that it's coming to Region VII, the National Training Conference.
Mr. Gary Blackmon: First, I would like to say I'm really sorry that the - - I hate to see the old Board members who are leaving because I have really learned to respect a lot of the things that – and the knowledge that they have, that they bring – brought with them when they came to the Board. And I tell you, it teaches you that when you think you know a whole lot when you're coming on the Board, it really is probably best to sit back and listen to what's being said with those who have the experience; and we're really losing a lot of experience.

And I want you to know from the bottom of my heart how much we have appreciated information and the challenges that you've brought for us and the things that you've done to bring us to the next level. And I will say to the new members that we have a long road ahead. Keep the faith. Keep your mind on the goals of the business of Blacks In Government and I think we'll be fine; and I welcome you on the Board. And finally, on another note, I would like to add that now is the time for us to think about the people who were affected by Katrina. Everyone else that rushed to do all of the things that they wanted to do, now is the time when we will see the results of the people who are affected and where they are going to need our help because that's – this is the time now, not when everybody else was jumping on the band wagon. So I would like you to think about that in the future. Thank you.

Mr. John Lyons: I would like to thank all of you for sharing your friendship with me while being on the Board, and I can say this has been really a learning experience, sitting on this Board over the years. I've sat here and I've seen things go, and I've seen thing come back again, the same way they went out. But, to the new members, I'm sure I've worked with some of you over a period of years. And I say welcome, bye, and next question.

Mr. J.B. Larkins: Well, you know, these few years that I've been with you, it's like it was yesterday. I was trying to, a while ago, to remember what I'm going to remember most about this Board. And I love all of you. But I think I love and remember Ellen Dyson more. The other thing that's most memorable is her fantastic memory. And, you know, I call her. I call her at home. Ellen, this happened about 20 years ago, can you tell me when – oh, that is on page so and so. And she will tell me who made the motion and who did the whole thing. That's really something to remember. So thank you Ellen. Thank all of you again for these few short years.

Mr. Charles Oliver: The Katrina and the Rita victims, we've been trying to work with them, and just trying to show more love because love, as the bible says, love is above all; and love can change all. So in saying that, I love all of you. Have a safe trip home.

Mr. Remond Henderson: I just want to say, like Ellen, this will be the first time in 21 years that I haven't been an officer in Blacks In Government; and she wants to find out what it's like afterwards. Well, I've found out, and it's been very lucrative. If you need some expert advice and consultation, you know how to get a hold of me. I want to thank one person that I think has done an outstanding job for the last few years that I've been on the Board and that is Ms. Cynthia Davis. She has done an outstanding job getting the minutes to us. She's prepared them in a professional manner. Some of you don't know how difficult it is to do that job, and to get this information to you in a timely manner. There are times when we had Board meetings and didn't have minutes by the time we closed. We still didn't have minutes. And I want to thank her for responding. Every time I called her to ask her for something, she has provided that. And she's always handled everything in a professional manner. And that's just the way I deal with things. And I also want to leave this room separating personal from business. I deal with business in this meeting, and when I walk out this door, we're friends. You know, some people cannot separate the two. It's not personal. It's not about me. It's not about you. Also, I want to thank Gerald Reed for the support I got from him when I was the Treasurer, and I want to thank him for raising my temperature level at times when he didn't support me. I wish Faye the best when she comes in as the Treasurer. It's a tough position. Abe can attest to that. If you take the job and do it in a professional manner and do things right, you will probably lose a few friends. But I know you can handle it. I wish all the new Board members coming on the board the best, and this is not how all Board meetings are. There were some difficult issues that we dealt with here and we talked about some issues that have been ignored for a while that needed to be discussed. So, I applaud the Board for at least taking some action and at least

bringing some things to the table, whether the action taken was appropriate, but at least you took some action. Anyway, I'll miss all of you. I really do miss the camaraderie. You don't know what it's like being in Alaska. Come and visit sometime. But I'm going to miss all of you from the bottom of my heart.
Mr. Gerald Reed: I would just like to, first off, thank the outgoing Board members for extending their knowledge base to assist us in making sure we keep Blacks In Government afloat, and look at your departure as a passing of progress. To the incoming Board members, just let it be known, you must put on your shoes because you will be running a race. And lastly, I would like to thank Rosa Louise Parks for sitting down to allow us to stand up and be accountable for Blacks n Government in our African American community at large. And to all, please have a safe and fruitful holiday season.
Mr. Abe Joseph: Since I've been – I really enjoyed – it's been very challenging serving on the Board for four years, and a total of 13 years at the national and regional levels. This is my first time not holding an office at any of those levels, which I'm very happy, and tickled to death. I do have really quite a lot of good friends. I learned a lot of stuff, and I'm here to support the new Treasurer, and I hope that this Board stand strong together, because we have got some – we've got a very challenging future ahead of us to maintain this organization, the solvency of it, and also the closeness that we need. To you new Board members, I don't know what you all are thinking about. But, I think you all are going to do a great job and I'm looking for some good things coming to Blacks In Government in the leadership role.
Ms. Darlene Young: To the outgoing Board members, I want to say thank you. When I came on this Board, many of you mentored me, gave me very good advice. Also helped me to be where I am today. To the incoming Board members, you have challenges that you will deal with as these Board members did that are leaving; but, I see that you all are active and anxious, because you raised your hands quite a bit for personal privilege,

and I think that's great because we know that you believe in Blacks In Government. And I think overall our organization has come a long way. It's been an interesting eleven months for me in this position. I have grown a lot and seen a lot, and I look forward to continuing to uphold the great standards of this organization. So I say to all of you, safe travels home, happy holidays, and I'll see you in January.
Mr. J. David Reeves: First of all, happy holidays to everyone in the coming days, and I pray that everyone has a very safe and prosperous new year. There are a lot of Board members that are leaving who I consider to be not just Board members, but friends. And I want to say to them thank you for your wisdom and your understanding and your knowledge and your patience; and it's hard to say good-bye to people you work so closely with. And in too many ways, I don't really consider it saying good-bye, because I know you'll be at the National Training Conferences, and I'll see you at BIG events; but it's a little different because we won't see you as frequently probably, and I want you to know that I love you all and I want to thank you all for all of the wisdom that you have. To the new Board members, I'm impressed. I think we've got a good crop, and I want to thank the regions for being wise enough to send us quality replacements form some of the vest and the brightest that we have. And even though we may be losing some really talented people, I think we've got some fresh new talent that's going to come on that's going to easily fill those shoes. And I think we have – we expect and anticipate big things from each of you. That's it.
Ms. Cynthia Davis: I just want to thank everyone for allowing the Central Arkansas, Greater Little Rock, and USDA Arkansas Chapters to host this particular meeting. We're sorry that we we're able to get out in Little Rock a little bit, but many of you don't know that the Clinton Library, this was the one year grand opening this week, and there were a lot of dignitaries and a lot of celebrities in town this weekend. And if any of you are leaving out tomorrow, I hope that you're able to at least stop by

and take a look at the facilities. It really is a beautiful facility inside. Maybe if some of you came across the interstate, you might have seen in it the distance, what we call our glorified trailer in the sky; but it really is nice on the inside. To the new incoming Board members, I want to offer my support as the National Secretary. If there is anything I can do for any of you, please don't hesitate to call me. And I want to echo some of the same sentiments as everyone else for the outgoing Board members. It has really been an experience working on the Board with you. If I could at least mention one person, and it's not disrespect to any of the rest of you, but I'm going to just go ahead on with it – it's Ellen Dyson. When I sat in Delegates Assembly all of those years and watched Ellen just go back and forth and do her Ellen thing, and I'm like who is this chick, you know, and you don't really understand her until I came to the Board. And I understand that she is about the business of Blacks In Government, and it didn't take me but one meeting to look at her and realize that, you know, it's like anybody would say, well, how is that Ellen Dyson, she's bad to the bone, She knows what she's talking about when she opens her mouth. And I have so much respect for you for that. And I think I learned a lot from her and all of you, and I thank you so much for just being there and being my inspiration to be able to continue with Blacks In Government. Thank you.

Ms. Lillian Barnett: I do believe – I think I still do believe that it's an honor to be on the Board. It's going to be a hard act for me to follow behind Ellen, but I'm going to give you my all. I'll give you my best. And I wish everyone to have a safe trip home.

Ms. Deborah Dawkins: Thank you so much for having us here. This really was very enlightening. And I just wanted to say to some of the people that are leaving the Board, I also know you in a different capacity, and I'm going to lose a couple of really good mentors. I know I'm not going to lose any friends, and I do have your numbers and your e-mails. Thank you.

Mr. Anthony Rhodes: Yes. Mr. Browne, Mr. Henderson, Mr. Larkins, Mr. Lyons, it's like the second time around for us. You guys – I said my goodbyes to these fellows one time before. But I do appreciate the opportunity to be here today to be able to see them as they depart, and I wish them the best luck, as well as the other Board members going out. To the current Board, I will be coming in January, ready to go to work, to try this again for a while. Thank you.

Mr. Palmer Doiley: I would like to thank Mr. Browne for his service and whose shoes I'll be trying to fill. I know about his long tenure and the hard work, but not all of the hard work that he's performed here. I certainly hope that I can begin to live up to the things that he brought to the Board, and I look forward to the challenge. And I'm sure that the fellow members that are coming on with me will be up to the task.

Mr. Alton Cochran: I'm not new to BIG, but I am new to the Board, and I really appreciated and thank my region for thinking enough to select me to replace Alma. Although, she has been informed that she's going to be holding my hand until I get set. So I will be here in January, hopefully, and may all of you have a happy holiday.

Ms. Mary Peoples: I must say it has been interesting to be a part of this Board. I've been fortunate to be able to see some old friends from the Board several years ago who are still here. (I'm) sad to say that I won't be able to serve with them again. It would be very much a challenge. And I would like to say that I'm like Lillian. I don't know whether to say it's an honor or not in a sense, but I'm up to the challenge. I wouldn't be here if it was not for my dedication to this organization because it is truly a supreme sacrifice that I am sitting here today. I would love to be at home in my yard - my passion for gardening. And BIG is the only organization I let supersede my passion for the things that I like to do. And I want to thank the Chair for inviting us to come and observe you in action today, and I look forward to being on the Board in January to do whatever I can to make BIG the best organization there is and to continue to be the best there is. And on behalf of all of our chapter members who look to you for guidance, you would be surprised that your reputation out there as a supreme organization. Stay that way. You would be surprised how a beacon of light you are to some people at state, local, and federal governments. I wish to all of you happy holidays and a safe trip back home, and I look forward to seeing the rest of you in January.

Ms. Toni Martin: I want to say happy holidays to all, and for those of you – a lot of you I do know and I must admit I am going to miss Ellen because she served with my husband and everything. So this is going to me a challenge. But in Region IX, we call JB the silver fox, and it is really doing to be heard not to be working side by side with JB, but now he'll be able to attack me at the regional meetings because I won't be able to vote now. So it will be interesting to work with JB in that capacity. I am excited about coming to the Board. After today, though, I was scratching my head a little bit, but I do believe in Blacks In Government, and I am very passionate about Blacks In Government. And I know that we still have a long way to go, but I know we'll get there. So I am excited. Happy holidays to all, and I'll see all of you guys in January, those that will be coming back. Thank you.

Ms. Faye Henderson: For all of my fellow Board members, as I have been a member of this body before, I'm going to miss you all. I've been, you know, even when I wasn't on the Board, I sat in on all of your meetings, so it still felt like I was part of the body anyway. I'm going to miss you a lot. I'm really going to miss Ellen because when I first came on the Board when everyone was telling me to be quiet and listen and learn, she told me to speak up. And because I was afforded the opportunity, I think it helped me grow, and here I am today. And I never even thought that I would be Treasurer of this organization - never even wanted it, as a matter of fact. But I do approach my new position with a lot of optimism, as well as some apprehension, too. I don't think I've slept well for the last – well, since I was elected; but I think about all of the things that I need to do and it just runs in my mind during the night. So it's difficult for me to sleep, but I just want everyone to know that I'm very dedicated to the position, and I'm going to give you my all; and I think we're going to be okay. I want to let my predecessors know that I appreciate them and the commitment that they made, and I will be looking to them for their knowledge, and I'm going to call you or track you down because I will need you; and I just want to say thank you because I know it really is an awesome commitment that you all have made, and you get beat up and you don't even get paid. So that's worth something in itself.

Ms. Kelly Brinson: It's been nice observing you guys. I came on my own to see how you all operate. I was at a workshop at the National Training Conference this year, and the workshop instructor made a statement that stuck with me, and it's become my motto. So I'm here to observe so when it's my time to step up to the plate, I'll be prepared.

Ms. Peggy Wilson: I want to thank everybody for letting me be the 2005 NTC chairperson. I really enjoyed it. It was a challenge, but I think that I did a fantastic job. And I also want to thank the people who appointed me as the National Evaluation Chair, and you will not be sorry for having me in that position. I will do my job and do my best. Thank you.

Mr. Oscar Williams: I make a motion that we adjourn.

Ms. C. Jacquie Beatty: Second.

Mr. Farrell Chiles: It's been moved by Mr. Williams and seconded by Ms. Beatty that we adjourn. It is now 11:14 p.m. The meeting is adjourned.

Chapter 9: Deployment 2004-2005

"The first step to leadership is servanthood." – John Maxwell

On May 13, 2004, I received mobilization orders to report to Fort Leonard Wood, Missouri on May 17, 2004. I was being deployed for 365 days in support of Operation Enduring Freedom. I asked for a seven-day extension and on the reporting date and began my travel. I drove my car and stopped nights in Flagstaff, Arizona, then Albuquerque, New Mexico, and Oklahoma City, Oklahoma. Just 70 miles outside of Fort Leonard Wood, near Springfield, MO on Interstate 40, I was stopped by a State Trooper for speeding. I showed him my driver's license and then produced my military orders bringing me on active duty. He replied, "They're taking old people now." He let me go without issuing a ticket. This was the first of three times that I was stopped for speeding while in Missouri. All three times, I did not receive a ticket. Priscilla Martin, a former co-worker of mine in California, now living in Missouri explained it to me, "The state troopers saw a Lexus automobile, with California license plates, a black man driving the car with a bald head. You were not just stopped for DWB (driving while black), but they thought you were a drug trafficker. When they pulled you over and saw an old man and found out that you were a military officer, they let you go. You were lucky."

While at Fort Leonard Wood, I stayed on the Board and continued to perform my duties as the Board Chair. Luck was on my side when I was assigned as the Chief of the Contingency Operations Team, with the responsibility to process all Soldiers going to and coming back from Theater, whether Iraq, Kuwait, or Afghanistan. My team consisted of sixteen civilians, mostly dependents or retired military personnel. The best part of the assignment was that I was a part of the Adjutant General's Office and the Directorate Head was Jesse French, a retired warrant officer, and an African-American. Jesse French was a consummate professional who talked, breathed, and slept his job. He was focused on successfully fulfilling the mission and was no-nonsense. He was very supportive of me. We both were warrant officers and knew some of the same people. Whenever I needed a three-day pass to conduct Black In Government's business, he always approved my request. While at Fort Leonard Wood, I did not miss a Board meeting and even attended other activities within the area. The post did not have a Black Employment Program (BEP) manager. This position is a collateral position and most often is filled by a civilian in the grade of GS-7 or higher. When word got around that the Chair of the Board of BIG was on post, even though I was on military status, I was asked to serve as the BEP manager. With the approval of my boss, I accepted. I recruited a committee and we designed a strategy to bring visibility to the program and increase the number of African-Americans at all levels at Fort Leonard Wood, which was much needed. I contacted Leonard Stone, BIG's webmaster and had Fort Leonard Wood's job vacancies listed on the BIGNET, BIG's website.

Blacks In Government had a chapter at Fort Leonard called the Central Missouri Chapter. What was unique about the chapter was it had its own office, a two story housing unit that had been converted to use for office space. The Chapter's president was Donald Reeves. I contacted him upon my arrival at Fort Leonard Wood. We met and I became a regular attendee at all of the chapter meetings and events. One weekend, we caravanned to Florissant, Missouri (near St. Louis) to attend a Region VII Council meeting and retreat. The retreat was held at a Catholic Monastery. The rooms were small and so were the beds. However, the meeting that weekend was very productive and everyone had a great time. But, there were no telephones or televisions. We had training sessions as well as the regional council meeting.

I also drove 420 miles to attend a Region V Council meeting at the Renaissance Hotel in Oakbrook, Illinois. The Regional Council President was Thomas Walton who also served as the Board's parliamentarian and the National Delegates Assembly Chair. The business was conducted in a very professional manner (that's Mr. Walton for you). The meeting was well-attended and most chapters had their designed three representative. After the meeting, the New Kemet Harambe Chapter hosted a reception. There was plenty of good food, good music, much fun, dancing, bid whist, and just a good time. I really enjoyed myself. I enjoyed being with my BIG family. And, I appreciated the way people accepted me and showed me their hospitality.

Prior to becoming a member of the Board, I had attended a Region XI Council meeting on a Saturday morning, while TDY in the Washington, D.C. in September 2000. Dawn Lawson picked me up at my hotel and escorted me to the meeting. Unlike most regions that hold quarterly meeting, Region XI holds monthly meetings. That was my first exposure to any regional meeting outside of my Region IX Council meeting. So, now I had experienced four different council meetings in different regions of the country. I did a mental analysis of each region. Each had its own personality and nuances and different ways of conducting its business. In the end, each region took care of the business of BIG and that was the key. There were dedicated people and devoted their weekends and time to ensure that their chapters were represented and that the goal and objectives were the focal point of the organization. They cared about making a difference and were willing to make the necessary sacrifices to conduct BIG's business. I was very proud of my association with the organization.

For Christmas 2004, I received a four day pass to go home for Christmas. But, I also had the week end off for the New Year's weekend. Dr. Doris Sartor, one of the Region IV Directors, invited me to Montgomery, Alabama to spend New Year's. I arrived at the Montgomery Airport and was met by the Chapter President, David E. Smith, Sr. We drove to a local restaurant and met other members of the General Chappie James Chapter. Chapter member Sandra Glenn was there with her two sons, Chad and Jayson, and we had great conversation and I felt the warm southern hospitality. During my visit, I stayed at the Maxwell Air Force Base in VIP Quarters. On New Year's Eve we went to a party at a nearby hotel sponsored by the Omega Psi Phi Fraternity and the BIG Chapter. I am not a partier and had not been up to see a new year come in since 1983. I had a difficult time staying awake and making conversation when most people were out on the dance floor having fun. I usually go to bed at 8:00 p.m. and would have if I weren't where I was. But, everyone had a good time. The next day, we all had a special lunch at the Martha's Place Restaurant owned by Martha Hawkins, a lady who was once on welfare. She started selling meals out of her house to get off welfare. Her story was featured in national magazines and she was once a guest on the Oprah Winfrey Show highlighting her success. The food was delicious. The restaurant is usually closed on New Year's Day, but in honor of me (maybe), she opened it just for our party. Ida Tyree-Hyche and her husband, Rev. Albert Hyche, the Presiding Elder of the AME Church in Birmingham, Alabama also joined us. Rev. Hyche gave one of the most inspiring prayers that I had ever heard. Ida Tyree-Hyche, a fellow warrant officer, federal employee, and BIG Life Member and I belong to several of the same organizations and she was one of my strong supporters. In 2004, she was actually my speech writer for the Delegates Assembly and National Training Conference.

During my stay at Fort Leonard Wood, I had free time most evenings and began to order books on-line from Barnes and Noble. I was a political science major in college and have always been fascinated by political figures and their lives. So I started ordering autobiographical and biographical books on African-American politicians – mayors, congressional leaders, and state representatives. I especially enjoyed the ones that shared their campaign strategies and how they won elections. I usually read 75 pages in the evening, seventy-five pages in the morning and another seventy-five pages the next evening. Most books were approximately 250 pages, so I'd complete a book within two to three days. By the time that I left Fort Leonard Wood, I had collected over one hundred books and had read every one of them.

Prior to the January 2005 Board meeting, I went to the Fort Leonard Wood Craft Shop and ordered one hundred 5" tall glasses engraved with the BIG Logo and the words: "Blacks In Government – Installation of National Officers – January 28, 2005 – Dean Acheson Auditorium – Washington, D.C.". The glasses were shipped to the Board of Directors' meeting hotel (the Embassy Suites) and arrived in time for distribution to Board members, Executive Committee members and others.

Chapter 10: The Final Year 2006

"Trust is the essence of leadership." – Colin Powell

Blacks In Government
National Board of Directors Meeting
Richmond Marriott Hotel
Richmond, Virginia
Friday, January 20, 2006

Excerpts from the official transcript:

Mr. Farrell Chiles: Good morning. It is January 20, 2006. The National Board of Directors of Blacks In Government, the meeting is officially called to order. The time is 9:10 a.m. I would like to start the session off with an opening prayer. Mr. Oliver, would you do us the honors, please?...

Mr. Farrell Chiles: The next item on the agenda is the election of the Board Chair, Vice Chair, and I've asked Mr. Walton to conduct the election. Mr. Walton.

Mr. Thomas Walton. We first would like to read to you the duties of the Chair of the Board of Directors in accordance with the National Constitution. "The Chair of the Board of Directors serve as Chair of the Board of Directors, officially transmits the policies which have been approved by the Board of Directors, recommends to the Board of Directors changes in policies and procedures, presents the organization's annual report to the annual Delegates Assembly, appoints committee chairs of the board with the consent of the board, and is an ex-officio member of the board committees; requires reports on the activities of the Regional Councils and the chapters -- through the Board of Directors from the regions and board committees; performs such functions and exercises such other authority as may be prescribed by the Board of Directors. The Chair of the board cannot be a member of the Executive Committee"…

Mr. Thomas Walton: At this time, the floor is open for nominations for the office of Chair of the National Board of Directors.

Mr. Oscar Williams: Oscar Williams, Region V. I nominate Farrell Chiles.

Mr. Thomas Walton: Farrell Chiles has been nominated. Are there any further nominations for the Office of Chair of the National Board of Directors? On second call, are there any further nominations for the office of Chair of the National Board of Directors? On third and final call. I see no hands; I hear no voices.

We declare the nominations closed on the name of Mr. Farrell Chiles.

(Applause)

Mr. Thomas Walton: Mr. Chair, the results of the election for Vice Chair: Mr. J. David Reeves has 13 votes; Ms. Angela Thorpe-Harris has 12. We declare Mr. J. David Reeves re-elected as the Vice Chair of the National Board of Directors of Blacks In Government.

(Applause)

Mr. J. David Reeves: Now, that's an election.

Mr. Thomas Walton: Mr. Chiles, would you stand please, and Mr. Reeves. Mr. Chiles and Mr. Reeves, you have been re-elected as Chair and Vice Chair of the National Board of Directors. Do you accept your election?

Mr. Farrell Chiles: I do.

Mr. J. David Reeves: I do.

Mr. Thomas Walton: We declare you officially re-elected into your positions. We ask that you would repeat after me.

"In accordance with Article VI of the National Constitution of Blacks In Government, and the National Board Policy, 3:07, I do affirm that I will to the best of my knowledge, skills, and abilities, adhere to the mandates of the National Constitution of Blacks In Government, the District of Columbia Code, and I will carry out the duties of the office to which I have been elected. All of this I do solemnly affirm."

To the Board members, I present you Chair and Vice Chair for the year 2006.

(Applause)

Mr. Farrell Chiles: On behalf of J. David and me, we would like to say thank you to the Board members for your faith in us for the year 2006.

The Board had approved the agenda with modifications. Prior to the election, I had moved to appoint Mr. Anthony Rhodes to fill the unexpired term of Dr. Doris Sartor for Region IV. Dr. Sartor had presented a letter of resignation from the Board of Directors effective December 31, 2005. At the 2005 National Delegates Assembly, she was elected to serve as the National Executive Vice-President. Mr. Rhodes was a previous Board Chair and a welcomed addition to the Board.

We received the President's Report. During the report, the National President yielded to Ms. Peggy Wilson, the 2005 National Training Conference Chair to provide a final conference report. Ms. Young then yielded to Ms. Alma Garlington, the 2006 NTC Chair, for a status report on the 2006 NTC. Later, Ms. Young moved that we go into Executive Session to discuss legal issues. After the Executive Session, we continued to receive the President's Report. Upon its completion, Charles Oliver moved, seconded by Palmer Doiley to accept the President's Report for information only. The motion carried.

The next item on the agenda was the appointment of Board committee chairs and members. I had established a structured two-tiered committee process for the various committees to ensure that no one individual would serve on more than two of the committees or be in attendance at any two meeting at the same time. Committees were structured to meet simultaneously at two-tiered intervals.

Tier One consisted of the Financial Advisory /Oversight Committee; Time and Place/Delegates Assembly; Personnel; and Constitution P& Policy, Policy. Tier Two consisted of the Awards Committee; Program Oversight; Strategic Planning; and Constitution & Policy, By-Laws. The Constitution & Policy, Constitution Committee was not a part of the tier system.

I appointed Gary Blackmon, chair of the Financial Advisory/Oversight Committee; Regina Kennedy, chair of the Time and Place/Delegates Assembly; Katherine Cage, chair of the Personnel Committee; Angela Thorpe-Harris, chair of the Constitution & Policy, Policy Committee; Johnita Pitts, chair of the Awards Committee; David Hampton, Program Oversight; Gerald Reed, Strategic Planning; Delores Ivy, Constitution & Policy, By-Laws; and J. David Reeves, chair of the Constitution & Policy, Constitution.

The Board accepted my committee chair appointments and we went into recess until the next day at 9:12 a.m. The Board continued to conduct the business of Blacks In Government and we finally adjourned at 8:50 p.m. on Saturday, January 21, 2006.

Board Meeting; April 21, 2006; Embassy Suites; Cleveland, Ohio.

The meeting was called to order at 9:10 a.m. Charles Oliver led us with an opening prayer. We received greetings from Ms. Loretta Beavers, president of the Lake Erie Chapter and Region V Second Vice-President. A quorum was established, a revised agenda approved, and the minutes of the previous meeting were approved with corrections. We then went about the business of Blacks In Government.

The next item on the agenda was the Executive Committee Report. Darlene Young, the National President, made several motions that were referred to respective Board committees for review and report back to the full Board. Ms. Young moved that Ms. Norma Samuel be appointed as the Assistant Treasurer to fill the unexpired term ending December 31, 2006.

The Board passed a motion to allow the Financial Advisory/Oversight Committee to act on its behalf to approve contracts for the 2006 National Training Conference. We also suspended several chapters for calendar year 2004 non-compliant IRS 990 financial reports.

The president provided the Board with a report on New Orleans. New Orleans had been devastated by Hurricane Katrina. The Board had selected New Orleans for the 2008 National Training Conference. Ms. Young, James Wilson of the National Staff, and Regina Kennedy,

Chair of the Time & Place/Delegates Assembly Committee, made a fact-finding trip to New Orleans to meet with city officials, tour the city, and talk to people on the street. They came back with a strong recommendation that we keep our contract with New Orleans.

J. David Reeves made a motion that we continue with our original plans to go to New Orleans in 2008 for our National Training Conference. The motion passed without any opposition.

We recessed for lunch at 12:38 p.m. and reconvened at 2:47 p.m. After a quorum was established, we immediately went into Executive Session to discuss legal issues. We had some lively discussions on issues that affected the entire organization. We had to make some tough decisions. And we did. We lasted in Executive Session until 5:09 p.m.

After returning to general session at 5:23 p.m., the Board went into recess until the next morning.

The Board reconvened at 9:18 a.m. the next day. After establishing a quorum, the first item on the agenda was the Treasurer's report. We accepted the report, subject to audit.

After the Treasurer's report, we received the various Board committees' reports and acted on a multitude of proposals and motions. One significant motion, from the Time & Place/Delegates Assembly Committee was a recommendation of the following cities as finalists for 2011 and 2012. For 2011 – in alphabetical order: Atlanta, Georgia; Boston, Massachusetts; and Washington, DC. For 2012 – Atlanta, Georgia; Detroit, Michigan; and Washington, D.C. The motion passed.

On Saturday afternoon, we had a working lunch. Mr. Donald J. Campbell, BIG member and former Director of the National Aeronautics and Space Administration Glenn Research Center at Lewis Field in Cleveland was our guest speaker and spoke on the principles of leadership.

Later in the afternoon, we again went in Executive Session to discuss personnel issues. We had a long day. The meeting adjourned at 8:49 p.m. We had received complimentary tickets to a Cleveland Cavaliers play-off game from the Cleveland Convention and Visitors Bureau. But, we were unable to use them. We had to conduct the business of Blacks In Government.

Board Meeting; August 18, 2006; Hilton New York Hotel; New York, New York

The meeting was called to order at 9:22 a.m. J. David Reeves led all assembled with an opening prayer. Ms. Joyce Jones, Region II Director, brought greetings on behalf of Region II. Ms Carmen Laracuente, New York Blood Center, brought remarks regarding the NTC Drive. A quorum was established, an amended agenda was approved, and the minutes approved as corrected. Mr. Philip Atwell brought greeting on behalf of the region.

The Constitution and Policy (By-Laws) Committee gave its report followed by reports from the Regional Directors. We recessed at 4:41 p.m. Board members were discharged to attend their respective committee meetings.

The Board reconvened on Saturday, August 19th at 9:37 a.m. Anthony Rhodes led all assembled in prayer. A quorum was established and we commenced to receive the President's Report.

The President moved for the removal of certain chapters from the suspension list as a result of their compliance with the requirement to file their calendar year 2004 financial reports and moved for the revocation of other chapters' charters for failure to file fiscal year 2004 financial reporting requirements. Both motions carried. The Board also approved the President's motion of the 2007 National Training Conference theme, "Meeting the Challenges of a Changing Work Environment." Ms. Young reported that BIG received a Pinnacle Award from the Empower Network in Houston, Texas on June 24th.

Ms. Alma Garlington, the 2006 NTC Chair, gave the Board an update of the status of the 2006 NTC and confirmed that the opening guest speaker was Congressman Charles Rangel of New York and the closing keynote speaker was Congresswoman Stephanie Tubbs Jones. She reported that we had 2,837 pre-registration conference attendees. Ms. Jacquie Beatty, the 2007 Conference Chair gave a report of the 2007 NTC.

Ms. Young introduced the Board to a new pilot program as an extension of the Officer Leadership Program. The pilot, named the Young Leadership Academy, was a collaboration between BIG and he

U.S.D.A. Graduate School. Modeled after the USDA leadership curriculum, this certified program received $15,000 in funding from Deloitte.

The Board accepted the President's Report and later received the Treasurer's Report and accepted that report subject to audit. The Board then recessed for lunch.

Committee reports were next on the agenda. Regina Kennedy, chair of the Time & Place/Delegates Assembly Committee was first to make a presentation. She moved by committee action, that the following cities be selected for the 2011 and 2012 National Training Conferences: 2011, Boston, Massachusetts; 2012, Detroit, Michigan. The motion carried.

Angela Thorpe-Harris, Chair, Constitution & Policy (Policy) moved to approve added language to Policy 1:20. The motion passed. She then moved for approval of added language to Policy 3:18, Annual Audit Information/Reporting-Exit Interview. The added language provided for at least one member of the FA/OC other than the National Treasurer and National President shall be present for the auditor's exit interview. The motion carried.

We then went into Executive Session to receive the Personnel Committee Report. We spent two hours in Executive Session.

Back in General Session, Gary Blackmon, Chair, Financial Advisory and Oversight Committee, introduced Ms. Dorothy Proctor of Bert Smith and Company to provide an overview of the audit report.

Ms. David Hampton, Chair of the Program Oversight Committee presented a proposal for a Blacks In Government/Federal Employees Education and Assistance Funds (FEEA) Scholarship Program. By committee action, she moved that the Board approve a three year pilot program with FEEA, starting in 2007, to provide scholarship opportunities for BIG members' dependent children and grandchildren. The motion carried.

The Board went into Executive Session again to discuss personnel issues. Throughout the week of the National Training Conference, the Board convened to discuss and act upon several "hot" issues. On Friday, August 25, 2009, at 9:50 p.m., we finally officially adjourned. It was a very long week.

Board Meeting; November 17, 2006; Embassy Suites Hotel; Seattle, Washington

The Board was called to order at 9:15 a.m. Mr. J. David Reeves led us in an opening prayer. Charles Oliver, Region X Director, brought greetings on behalf of Region X. In addition to the Board members, the eight newly elected Board members for 2007 were in attendance. The agenda was approved as amended. The minutes of August 18-25, 2006 were approved as corrected.

Darlene Young, the National President, presented the Executive Committee's Report. By Committee action, Ms. Young moved that the Region II Council receive $25,000, representing a percentage of the total net conference revenue in accordance with Board Policy. The motion carried.

The Board approved $10,000 to fund the Young Leadership Academy. A preliminary report on NTC 2006 was received. Estimated revenue of $1,603, 968 and estimated expenses of $1,279,300 was provided to the Board. The report was accepted for information only. The Board went into Executive Session at 4:18 p.m. until 5:43 p.m. Board members were discharged to attend committee meetings for the rest of the evening.

We reconvened on Saturday morning, November 18th. During the course of the meeting, we received the Treasurer's Report. The report was accepted subject to audit.

The Constitution & Policy (Policy) made several motions for approval of changes to Board policies. Affected policies included Policy 1:08; Policy 2:01; Policy 2:18, Policy 1:16, and Policy 1:23. They were all approved.

The Financial Advisory/Oversight Committee presented the FY 2007 for approval. After much discussion and amendments, the budget was approved as amended.

The Board voted to direct the National Executive Committee to re-energize the Winning Ways Program which had been in an inactive status for some time.

We approved the revised by-laws of the Lake Erie Chapter, Cereal City Chapter, and the Norfolk Naval Shipyard Chapter. We approved the charters of two new chapters – Capitol Chapter and BIG-Southeast Wisconsin Chapter.

The Personnel Committee, chaired by Katherine Cage, by committee action moved for the approval of the national office vacancy announcements with timelines. The motion carried. This was a very controversial motion. The Board had approved a motion to restructure the National Office with new positions and job descriptions. Procedures were put in place. A Personnel/Selection Committee was authorized to act on behalf of the Board in the selection of applicants to fill the staff positions related to the national office vacancy announcements. This action did not finalize, as the new Board in 2007 rescinded the action

Because both the Chair and Vice-Chair's terms of office ended on December 31, 2006, there was discussion on the succession of the January 2007 meeting of the Board. A motion was made to allow the National Secretary to conduct the January 2007 Board Meeting until the elections were completed. The motion carried.

Mr. Oscar Williams moved, seconded by Mr. Gary Blackmon, to adjourn. The motion carried. The meeting was adjourned at 11:07 p.m. I hit the gavel for the last time.

PART TWO

Presenting Kathrene Hansen, Executive Director, Greater Los Angeles Federal Executive Board, with the Los Angeles/Long Beach Area Chapter's Public Service Recognition Award in Long Beach, CA (May 2000).

With past National Presidents Ramona McCarthy and Rubye Fields at NTC 2000 in Washington, DC at the Marriott Wardman Park Hotel - August 2000.

With Autry Adams, Agency Head, U.S. Customs – Long Beach, CA and J.B, Larkins, National Board of Directors. Presented Ms. Adams with the Los Angeles/Long Beach Area Chapter's Federal Agency Public Service Recognition Award in May 2000.

With Bishop Vashti McKensie, the Opening Plenary speaker, at the NTC 2004 in Washington, DC (Aug. 2004).

POW Shoshana Johnson and Congresswoman Diane E. Watson at the Jackie Robinson American Legion Hall, Los Angeles, CA – June 6, 2003.

With Shoshana Johnson at Press Conference during NTC 2004 in Washington, DC at the Marriott Wardman Park Hotel – August 2004.

With Gerald R. Reed, BIG National President, at the Atlanta Hilton Hotel during NTC 2002 in Atlanta, Georgia (August 2002).

In Orlando, Florida, with Orlando City Commissioner, Daisy W. Lynum (August 2005).

With Rebecca Lewis, my Executive Assistant. at the National Training Conference 2003 in Denver, Colorado (August 2003).

Participants at the Governance In America Program at NTC 2004 in Washington, DC(left to right) - J.W. Scarborough (National Association of Black County Officials); Danny Davis (Congressman, Illinois); Harvy Johnson (National Conference of Black Mayors); Farrell J. Chiles (BIG - National Board Chair); Gregg Reeves (BIG - National President): John Gage (American Federation of Government Employees - National President); and Webster Guillory (National Organization of Black County Officials -National Board Chair). (August 2004).

Meeting with the first African American mayor of Pine Bluff, Arkansas, the Honorable Carl A. Redus, Jr. (March 2005).

Addressing luncheon attendees at Victor's Hideout Restaurant in St. Thomas, USVI, in December 2005.

Group photo with Governor Charles W. Turnbull of the U.S. Virgin Islands at the Governor's Reception in December 2005.

With NASCAR driver and champion Jimmy Johnson at the CBS "The Early Show" in New York City during NTC 2006 (August 2006).

With Harry Smith, co-host of "The Early Show" in New York City during NTC 2006 (August 2006).

With Rene Syler, co-host of the CBS "The Early Show" in New York City during NTC 2006 (August 2006).

With Kweisi Mfume, NAACP President, at the NAACP Annual Convention in Baltimore, Maryland (July 2000).

Photo with Admiral Thad W. Allen, Coast Guard Commandant, at the 98th NAACP Annual Convention in Detroit, Michigan (July 2007).

Sitting in Army Reserve duty office in Los Alamitos, CA - September 2006.

Group photo with luncheon attendees during Leadership Excursion in Hawaii (December 2006).

With Congressman Danny Davis at the NTC 2007 Legislative Luncheon at the Gaylord Hotel in Nashville, Tennessee (August 2007).

Holding the Greater Los Angeles Federal Executive Board's Distinguished Public Service Career Award (May 2007).

Honoring Maycie Herrington (left) and Autrilla Scott (right) at the BIG Greater Orange County Chapter's "Tribute to Black Women" luncheon in Los Alamitos, CA (March 2008).

Accepting a Department of Defense Certificate of Appreciation from Clarence Johnson, Principal Director and Director for Civilian Equal Opportunity, Office of the Deputy Under Secretary of Defense (Equal Opportunity) at NTC 2007 in Nashville, Tennessee (August 2007).

Radio Celebrity Tom Joyner at the Tuskegee Airmen Inc.'s annual banquet at the Gaylord Texan Hotel in Grapevine, Texas (August 2007).

With Tennessee State Senator Thelma Harper at the NTC 2007 Legislative Luncheon at the Gaylord Hotel in Nashville, Tennessee in August 2007.

With Tim Russert, Host of "Meet the Press", at the Greater Washington, DC Boys and Girls Club's annual Legislative Dinner, April 2007.

Chapter 11: Brown v. Board of Education February 2004

The California AARP had an African-American Initiative and I met the state coordinator - Mrs. Nita Jones. She invited me to a Friday kick-off luncheon in Oakland at the downtown Marriott Hotel. I also received an invitation to another event the next evening at Merritt College sponsored by an organization of African-American Telecommunications professionals. I found out that the Bay Area Black Lawyers Association was having a function at the Oakland African-American Library & Museum that Saturday and Linda Brown Thompson (Brown v. Board of Education) was the guest speaker. I looked forward to attending the event.

The AARP luncheon was well-attended by invitees and I enjoyed the meeting African Americans involved in AARP. It was an eye opener for me. I was a member of AARP (yes, I am over 50). I didn't know so many African American were actively engaged in the leadership of the organization. The kick-off was a success.

The next day, I attended the Black lawyers' event with the Damita Barbee, National President of the Urban Financial Services Coalition (UFSC). The presentation was excellent and provided a different perspective on the historic case. At the end of the presentation, Ms. Brown Thompson took a couple of questions and left before the event was over. We had time to kill before the next event at Merritt College, so we decided to have a late lunch at the Claremont Hotel in Berkeley. Upon arriving at the hotel, I went browsing in the Gift Shop for a souvenir key chain and saw Linda Brown Thompson in the shop. I approached her and said that I had followed her from downtown Oakland to the hotel. I don't know whether she believed me or not, but she knew that I was where she was before she arrived at the hotel and I knew the details of her presentation. It was just luck that she was staying at the hotel where we decided to go to and have lunch. I told her that I was with Blacks In Government and would like for her to speak at an upcoming event in Los Angeles. She gave me the name and phone number of her agent and we parted ways.

On the following Monday, I called her agent and he said that he was expecting my call. Ms. Brown Thompson had called ahead. We discussed possible dates and fees and would eventually sign a contract for Ms. Brown Thompson and her sister, Ms. Cheryl Brown Henderson, to speak at a Los Angeles/Long Beach Area Chapter fundraiser in celebration of the Brown v. Board of Education Supreme Court decision. The Year 2004 was the 50th anniversary of the decision.

The Los Angeles/Long Beach Area Chapter submitted a Monetary Assistance Program (MAP) application to the National Executive Committee that was approved. The chapter's Programs Committee, chaired by Carolyn Adams, went about ensuring that the program would be a success. The luncheon was held on October 21, 2004 at the Westin (Airport) Hotel in Los Angeles. For the Mistress of Ceremonies, the chapter got Dr. Erylene Piper Mandy, who was the Opening Plenary speaker at the 2003 National Training Conference in Denver.

Unfortunately, I was unable to attend the event. In May 2004, I received my orders for a one year mobilization in support of Operation Enduring Freedom. I was at Fort Leonard, Missouri when the event occurred. During the program, Carolyn Adams mentioned my name and thanked me for my leadership in the preliminary stages of arranging the celebration and the event.

Chapter 12: Re-election Campaign 2004 – Board of Directors

On June 16, 2004, at 10:08 a.m. (cst), I sent the following e-mail to Region IX chapter presidents.

From: Chiles, Farrell
Subject: Candidacy for Board of Directors
Sent: 614/04 10:08 a.m.

To All,

I am officially announcing my candidacy for the National Board of Directors representing Region IX. I ask for your support and vote.

Thank you for Continuing to Think BIG.
Farrell J. Chiles
Chair, National Board of Directors
Blacks In Government

At 1:54 p.m. (pst), Ken Pearson sent his e-mail:

To my BIG Family

This is the official announcement of my candidacy for BIG National Board of Directors from Region IX. I request your vote to continue serving all of Region IX.

Kenneth Pearson
Region IX Council Immediate Past President

At 3:41 p.m. (pst), Earl Bryers responded with his e-mail:

Hello Fellow BIG Members,

This is the official announcement of my plan to run for BIG National Board of Directors position from Region IX. I request your vote and promise to serve you, the members of Region IX to the best of my ability.

Please be advised that this is a last minute decision on my part. I humbly seek your support for this very important position in our region.

Sincerely,
Earl L. Bryers,
2nd Vice-President, Region IX
Blacks In Government
and Immediate Past President,
Greater San Diego Chapter

I sent Ken Pearson an e-mail message:

Hello Mr. Pearson!
//Farrell

He responded:

Hello Mr. Chiles!!
KP

I sent Earl Bryers an e-mail:
Earl,
Welcome to the race!
//Farrell

I received a reply from Earl:

Thanks Farrell,
Call me or I'll call you to explain why I made the decision to run.
Take Care!
Earl

Later the same day, I sent an e-mail to my campaign manager, La Fonda Frazier:

Hi LaFonda / Ms. Campaign Manager,

There are three (3) people in the race as of today – Myself, Kenneth Pearson and Earl Bryers. My campaign strategy is to ignore both of them and confirm that Toni Martin is supporting me. She indicated in April that I had her support. I need to keep it.

We don't need to talk to anyone else, but Toni. With Toni's supporting me, others will follow. Make sure Toni Martin loves me!

Thanks.

//Farrell

Irene Haynes from the Inland Empire Chapter sent me an e-mail:

Hello Farrell,

It seems you have two so far wanting your position!! My vote is for you.

Irene Haynes

I responded to Irene.

Hi Irene,

Thanks for the response. I don't mind the competition as long as I win.

With your support and others who have indicated that they will vote for me, I feel very confident (but cautious, that I will win). Please talk to your chapter and Assembly delegates and ask them to vote for me.

Talk to you soon.

//Farrell

J. B. Larkins, my mentor and fellow Board members sent me an encouraging e-mail.

> Everything is gonna be alright. Keep the faith.
> J.B.

I received an encouraging e-mail from Eddie Royal, Sr., President of the Los Angeles Civic Center Chapter:

> Hello Farrell,
> You have it from the Los Angeles Civic Center Area Chapter. You are in!!
> Eddie

Others sent me e-mails of support. My goal was to win with 60% of the vote.

On July 14th, I picked up my 5x7 three color gloss stock election cards from the local printing company and mailed a hundred of them to La Fonda Frazier for distribution at the upcoming Regional Council meeting, that I was unable to attend.

2004 Re-election; Delegates Assembly; Washington, D.C.

In my reelection to the Board in 2002, I had no opposition. But, that was not the case in 2004. I had two worthy opponents. Ken Pearson was the past Regional Council President and Earl Bryers was the Greater San Diego Chapter President. I signed my nomination papers and went about campaigning to win the election. Again, I had the numbers on my side. The Los Angeles/Long Beach Area Chapter had sixteen delegates. I had the support of several other delegates from other chapters. But to seal the deal, I wanted the support of Toni Martin and the Sacramento Metro Chapter. On Saturday evening, prior to Delegates Assembly, I hosted a reception for the chapter in my suite (the Marriott Wardman Park Presidential Suite). I had some food catered in and some prepared in the suite's kitchen.

Each morning, I met with my Election Team for breakfast in my suite. LaFonda Frazier served as my campaign manager and others on the team were Priscilla Martin, Carolyn Adams, and Irene Haynes, President of the Inland Empire Chapter. Also in attendance was my Executive Assistant, Rebecca Lewis. We would identify each chapter in attendance and their delegates. La Fonda Frazier's mission was to ensure that she stayed in touch with Toni Martin and deliver her votes. I believe that she may have actually sat next to her during the entire Delegates Assembly sessions. Region IX had a total of 48 delegates. In the end, I was re-elected with 60.4% of the vote. I received 29 votes; Ken Pearson received 16 votes; and Earl Bryers had 3 votes. Because of term-limits, this election would be my last as a candidate for the Board of Directors.

Chapter 13: Visiting Chapters

In October 2004, while attending an annual meeting of the United States Army Warrant Officers Association in Gettysburg, PA, the National Institute of Health (NIH) Chapter was hosting an event and I woke up early and drove to Bethesda, Maryland. In the absence of the National President, I signed a Memorandum of Agreement (MOA) with the agency head. The document later appeared in an issue of the Congressional Record. Several students won awards for their participation in an essay contest sponsored by the chapter.

On another occasion, while attending an Executive Committee meeting in Washington, DC, I slipped away to the Defense Intelligence Agency (DIA) for a chapter membership rally. I remember the event because it was first time that I received a certificate of appreciation from a chapter. The DIA Chapter is very special chapter for me.

I was in San Antonio, Texas attending a Combined Federal Campaign regional workshop and called the local BIG chapter president. He picked me up at my hotel, took me by his house, gave me a tour of his church, and then we met another chapter member and had lunch at a local soul food restaurant.

On my way to Fort Leonard Wood, Missouri, I stopped to spend one night in Albuquerque, New Mexico and had dinner with the National Corresponding Secretary, Angela Harvey, who had recently re-located in the area. We had great conversation and the food was excellent.

Again, while attending a military conference in St. Petersburg, Florida, I was picked up at my hotel by a Bay Area Chapter member, Gwendolyn Sanderlin. We had a good conversation and she shared with me that she had recently became her agency's first Information Technology (IT) specialist to receive the NOAA Employee of the Month. I was introduced to the chapter president, LeVerne Feaster, and was given a brief tour of her work place at the Veterans Hospital. I attended the chapter's monthly meeting and later joined several chapter members and went to a nice Jamaican restaurant. We had fun talking, laughing, and sharing with each other about our experiences in BIG.

In DC on business, on February 16, 2005, I found time to attend an installation of officer's ceremony with the National President at the Financial Management Service (FMS) Chapter. The chapter president, Pat Lee, organized the ceremony and the reception that followed. It was another time to fellowship with BIG members, in addition to meeting the FMS Deputy Commissioner Ken Papaj, other non-BIG members, and having the opportunity to promote Blacks In Government.

I believed as Chair that my constituents were my fellow Board members. They were the ones that elected me to my prestigious position. However, I considered myself as a members' Chair and tried to connect and stay connected with the entire BIG membership. Through my articles in the BIG Reporter - to my visits to chapters, I endeavored to show my interest in our members and how much I cared for each member.

Chapter 14: King Holiday January 2005

For the Dr. Martin Luther King, Jr. holiday weekend, I flew to Atlanta for four days. I mentioned the trip to MAJ Edgar Terry and he decided to meet me in Atlanta. Major Terry was deployed along with me to Fort Leonard Wood (FLW). After his one year tour at FLW, he volunteered for an assignment in IRAQ. MAJ Terry visited me in my office one day and noticed my BIG Life Membership plaque. We started talking about the many organizations to which I belong and I mentioned that I was a Life member of the ROCKS, Inc., an organization of Black military officers formed to provide mentoring and support for each other and junior officers. So, while at FLW we revitalized the local ROCKS chapter and he served as Acting President while he was stationed at FLW.

My hotel of choice in the Atlanta area is the Airport Embassy Suites. The chef makes a great serving of grits. On the holiday, we drove to the King Center, toured the museum and the book store, and later went to the auditorium for a book signing by Coretta Scott King, Bertha King, and Dr. King's sister, Florence King. We were not one of the early birds to arrive, so I showed my BIG business card to the usher and we were escorted to the front (second row). I had bought three books on Dr. King (one each for me, my daughter, and my granddaughter). While Ms. King was signing my books, I told her that I'd see her next month in Denver.

I was born in Greenville, South Carolina, so one day I made the two hour drive to visit relatives there. Upon returning to Atlanta, I had dinner with friends and the next day returned to FLW.

Every year during Black History Month, the Southwest Missouri sponsors an event in the community center for a performance of the St. Louis Black Repertory Theatre. I bought ten tickets and invited my boss and his wife. I was on the program for a brief presentation on the history of BIG. The reparatory play was fantastic.

The performance was well-attended. The event is one of the major fund-raisers for the chapter.

Delores Ivy, Board member from Region VII, invited me to a Black History Month event sponsored by the St. Louis Metro Chapter. The chapter had a one day training conference at a Hilton Hotel by the Airport. I arrived late and sat in the back. The keynote speaker was Norman Seay, a well-known activist and community leader in the St. Louis area. Mr. Seay served as the National Executive Vice-President of BIG in its early years and was the Chair of the first National Training Conference. Ms. Ivy introduced Mr. Seay to me and we had a wonderful conversation. I had read about him in some BIG documents, but also in former Congressman William Clay's book, "Only Permanent Issues." There was a reception afterwards and I got to talk to many of the attendees – both BIG members and government employees.

Later in the month, I flew to Denver for an annual program sponsored by the Denver Federal Executive Board (FEB). This event was at a local hotel and had 900 people in attendance. I arrived a day early, and the members of Region VIII had a dinner reception for me and the National President who was also attending the event. The keynote speaker for the FEB program was Ms. Coretta Scott King. I did not get to attend the reception in honor of her prior to the program and thus was not able to say "good seeing you, again."

I had made contact with Steve Bauer, the Executive Director of the Federal Employee Education & Assistance Fund (FEEA) located in Lakewood, Colorado. I had a concern that among sixty winners of the National Active and Retired Federal Employees (NARFE) Scholarship Fund that's administered by the FEEA, none were Black students. I wanted to talk to him about how BIG and the FEEA could work together to assist Black students in obtaining scholarships. We agreed to meet at the FEB event. I, along with Sandra Johnson, President of the Denver Mile Hi Chapter, met with Steve and had a good discussion. Mr. Bauer agreed to attend a future Board meeting and make a presentation on how BIG and the FEEA could collaborate to increase the number of Black students receiving scholarships. He promised to write a letter of introduction to the Board's Program Oversight Committee Chair and provide background information about the FEEA.

It was a good trip.

Chapter 15: Barack Obama February 2005

In February 2005, I was in Washington, D.C. attending a conference. I decided to take a taxi and go by the Dirksen Senate Office Building and make a call on the country's newest Senator – Barack Obama. His transitional office was located on the basement level and was not up to par with other Senate offices that I had visited in the past. I introduced myself to the receptionist and gave her my BIG business card. I asked for a future appointment with Senator Obama. She told me that I would be contacted within two weeks.

An appointment was made for the next time that I was in the DC area. I contacted Darlene Young, BIG's new President and asked her to join me in the meeting. By the time of the appointment, Senator Obama's office location had moved to the Hart Senate Office Building. Much better! We were not able to meet with the Senator but did meet with his Legislative Director, Chris Lu. Mr. Lu was Obama's Harvard Law School classmate and had been a congressional committee staff member prior to his new position. Luckily, he had heard of Blacks In Government and we had a discussion on some of the issues that was on the forefront of BIG's agenda. We left some BIG literature with Mr. Lu and a letter inviting Senator Obama to be a keynote speaker at our 2005 National Training Conference. Sometime later in the year, we received correspondence that Senator Obama would be unable to attend the conference.

That year, at the Congressional Black Caucus Foundation's Legislative Conference, I was able to get tickets for the Annual Awards Dinner. I invited my Executive Assistant, Barbara Johnson Cox, as my guest. During the dinner's intermission, Barbara walked around the banquet room and returned with a photo of her and Obama. She was one up on me.

In October 2006, I was in Tampa, Florida attending a conference and found out that Senator Obama would be making a book signing event in Los Angeles. However, you had to purchase his book,

"The Audacity of Hope" from a specific African American book store in order to be admitted to the signing which was being held at the California African American Museum (CAAM). I called J.B. Larkins and asked him to go by the bookstore and purchase two books for me. He met me at the event and I stood in line and got both books signed. I didn't have a camera that day, so I was not able to get a photo-op. I did have the foresight to purchase three "Obama for President" campaign buttons from an unauthorized vendor, although the Senator had not announced his intent to seek the office.

Less than four months later, Senator Obama announced that he was running for the Democratic Party nomination for President of the United States of America.

Chapter 16: As Long as There is Government – There Will Be – Blacks In Government

In preparation of the 2005 Delegates Assembly and the National Training Conference, I e-mailed Barbara Johnson Cox, my Executive Assistant, a list of the several tasks that we needed to complete prior to those events.

Ms. Johnson Cox, an excellent speech writer, asked me to provide a theme and speaking points that I wanted to cover in my speeches. For the National Training Conference Opening Plenary Session, I wrote a draft of the first paragraph and the last paragraph, and she did the rest. For the closing, I came up with a catchy phrase: "As long as there is government, there will be, Blacks In Government". I hoped that the phrase would catch on with the organization, just as the phrase, "Thank You for Thinking BIG had. That phrase has had a lasting effect and everyone is familiar with it and uses it quite often – whether on official stationary, at the end of an e-mail, or at the end of a conversation. It's part of the fabric of Blacks In Government. I hoped the same for my phrase. However, as Board Chair, I was not the decision-maker of what goes on the web page or on BIG's official literature. But, on every piece of information that I penned – my BIG Reporter messages, the Annual Corporate Reports, and my speeches, they all included the phrase – "As Long as There is Government – There Will Be – Blacks In Government".

The first introduction of the phrase came during my speech at the 2005 NTC Opening Plenary Session. I also used the phrase in my message to the attendees that appeared in the souvenir booklet. The essence of the phrase means that "the struggle continues." We must always remain vigilant. We must never let up – that BIG will always remain relevant. Just like any business, we are an ongoing entity and here for the long haul. BIG has a niche. We have value. We represent African-Americans in all sectors of public service and serve an advocate for them. As long as the United States exists, there is a role for BIG.

Slogans are very important to an organization. They help define them and what they are about. They help in the marketing of an organization and provide an identity for others to connect with them.

I wanted the phrase to serve a reminder and warning to all levels of government, that we are a player at the table. The phrase received a positive response that year. I heard others quote it in their presentations and conversations. I would start the phrase and let others end the sentence.

In using the phrase, I broke one of my rules. I used the word "be". It's a word that I try to avoid in my conversations and writings. "Be" is a passive word. It's also associated as a stereotype of African-American speaking patterns. But, in the end, I believed that the word was appropriate for the phrase.

I don't know how I came up with the phrase. I'm sure it's a variation of something that I had read before. Or maybe, there is a creative side of me that came through just at the right time. I just don't remember. But, one thing I know: "As Long as There is Government – There Will Be – Blacks In Government".

Chapter 17: Trip to the Defense Supply Center Philadelphia (DSCP)

I flew into National Airport (D.C.), staying at the Doubletree Hotel in Crystal City to attend a two day meeting of another non-profit organization that I served on its Board of Directors. Prior to attending the meeting, I had sent an e-mail to the National President and the two Regional Directors that I would be in the area. I received a phone call from Darlene Young about a trip she was making to Philadelphia to present an award to an agency and asked me if I would like to go. I said yes. Ms. Young picked me up early on the morning of January 12, 2006 and we drove to Union Station. We boarded an AMTRAK train (business class) and made the one and half hour trip to Philadelphia. This was my first ever ride on an AMTRAK train. We were met at the Philadelphia station and driven to the Defense Supply Center Philadelphia (DSCP).

Upon arrival, we were met by our host, the EO manager, and given a tour of the facility. Prior to going to the awards ceremony, we were greeted by Brigadier General Jesse R. Cross, the Commanding General and his staff. Our presentation was the first on the program. Blacks In Government presented the General and DSCP with a plaque in recognition of the agency's support of our programs and its donation of computers to the Janice M Scott Technology Center. Ms. Young, Johnita Pitts, Region III Director, Carol Bruce, Region III Council President, and Linda Bouie, project manager of the Janice Scott Technology Center were in attendance representing BIG at the event. We took photos that later appeared in the Spring issue of the BIG Reporter. Afterwards, I was dropped off at the Philadelphia International Airport for a Southwest Airlines flight back to California. It was a good trip.

Chapter 18: Trip to the Virgin Islands

In the early part of September 2005, I decided that I would like to take a trip to the Virgin Islands. I called Carson Edwards, Director of National Accounts, Marriott National Group Accounts, Marriott Global Sales Organization. While at the NTC in Orlando, Florida, I had met Carson and we had went off–site one afternoon and had lunch with excellent conversation. I was impressed with the young man. So, I wanted to send some business his way. He put me in contact with a senior account executive for Marriott and Renaissance Caribbean & Mexico Resorts and a contract was worked out. I had a flyer designed and advertised (via the BIGNET) a five day trip to St. Thomas. Several BIG members responded favorably to the advertisement and by the cut-off date I had a party of twelve for the trip. BIG members making the trip included Roxanna Beattie from Virginia; Mary Thomas, BIG Pentagon Chapter; Amicitia Maloon-Gibson, Southwest Missouri Chapter; Tonya Davis, Los Angeles/Long Beach Area Chapter; and Rowmell Hughes, Los Angeles/Long Beach Area Chapter. Also joining me on the trip was my daughter, Tracy Chiles McGhee, a D.C. attorney and her former co-worker and friend Jessica Knox, CEO of the Institute of Community Development (ICD), located in New Orleans, LA.

I contacted Ms. Thelma Santiago Brewster of the USVI Department of Tourism located in Los Angeles and she provided me with brochures and other information on the Virgin Islands and sent copies of the Islands' "This Week" magazine. Amicitia Maloon-Gibson, a native of St. Thomas, assisted with some of the logistics and with her in the party we would get a personal taste of the intricacies of the Island's history and culture.

On December 7, 2005, we arrived at the St. Thomas airport, met each other, and had the contracted van driver take us to the Marriott Frenchman's Reef Hotel. We checked into the hotel and that evening we had dinner at "Coco Joe's Off the Beach Bar", a restaurant at the hotel. The food was excellent and we enjoyed the live entertainment.

The next morning, we had breakfast in a meeting room reserved the entire week for us. Joining us at the meeting was Mr. Edouard de Lagarde, Chief of Staff from the office of U.S Congressional Delegate Donna M. Christiansen and Brigadier General Eddy L Charles, Sr., Adjutant General of the Virgin Islands and head of Homeland Security. Each spoke to us on their roles and gave informative overviews of the U.S. Virgin Islands. Later that day, we had lunch at the Victor's Hideout Restaurant with approximately fifteen local government employees. I had received sponsorship for each to receive a complimentary one year membership in BIG.

After lunch, we went to a reception at the Governor's mansion, where we met Governor Charles Turnbull, the Lieutenant Governor, Commissioners and other officials while enjoying the view from probably the highest point on the island. The reception had been coordinated by Barbara Johnson Cox, my Executive Assistant, working with the Governor's Protocol Office. Schedules were re-arranged and the Governor graciously hosted the reception and we shared information and met some wonderful people. The Governor was very supportive of Blacks In Government and we were honored by his hospitality and accommodations for our visit.

Later that day in the evening, we had light food, champagne, and good conversation in my suite before going our separate ways.

Each morning at 7:00 a.m. we had a morning walk. The first day, everyone showed up. After that, just Mary Thomas and I did this morning exercise. Either the time was too early, the walk too difficult, or others did their exercise on their own.

On Friday morning, we went on a tour of St. Johns. We took a 15 minute ferry ride for the two hour tour that cost us each $16.00. That evening most of us had dinner together at one of the hotel restaurants.

Saturday was a free day. Everyone did their own thing. I went to the town center, walked around, did some window shopping, dropped off some mail at the post office, met with postal workers and provided BIG literature for their perusal. I had a brief meeting with the postmaster in his office. I then went to outdoor bazaar/flea market. Later, I lay out on the beach and relaxed. We capped off our stay on our last evening on the island with dinner at the "Blue Beard's Castle"

Restaurant which had an excellent view of the Island that looked spectacular at night.

We were able to have fun, relax, conduct business, vacation, take a tour, and spread the name of Blacks In Government throughout the United States Virgin Islands. It was a good trip.

Chapter 19: Board Self-Assessment

I have served on several boards of directors. I served on BIG's Board for six years. Those six years were equal to the six years that I served on the Combined Federal Campaign's Orange County Local Federal Coordinating Committee (LFCC). None of the boards had ever done an assessment of functions and achievements. Such an assessment is highly encouraged by Board Source, an organization dedicated to providing training to increase the effectiveness on nonprofit organizations by strengthening their board of directors.

On January 3, 2006, I e-mailed the following message to current and outgoing Board members:

Thank you for your service on the Board of Directors and your exemplary leadership to the National Organization of Blacks In Government. Because of you, 2005 was a successful year. We look forward to even higher expectations for 2006.

Your input and insight are invaluable assets to BIG. I ask that you share your thoughts, suggestions, and ideas on improving the operational efficiency of the Board for 2006 and beyond. Please complete the assessment tool (attached), and return it back to me by January 13, 2006. I will arrange feedback to you. Consider, as you make your comments, BIG's mission and vision.

The assessment consisted of 23 questions:

1. Are there too many committees?
2. Do we need to redefine any committees?
3. Should the committee's and region's reports be submitted prior to the board meeting?
4. How should committee chairs and members be selected?
5. What other comments do you have to help improve the committees?

6. How can we improve the efficiency of the Board meetings?

7. Should we give advance notice on motions that will come before the board?
8. What should the function of the Thursday evening round table discussions be?
9. Should we have a working lunch on Saturdays? Is it relevant? Is it too costly?
10. What time should we start on Fridays?
11. How should we determine where we meet?
12. Does it matter what hotel chain we hold our board meetings?
13. How can we improve board communications between board meetings?
14. To what extent is the BIG mission of the organization clear, well-understood by all?
15. What would you say are the most important things the Board should be focusing on?
16. Overall, what would you say are the three most critical issues or questions to address in the next three to five years?
17. What would you say are the unique aspects of BIG that need to be reserved?
18. How satisfied are you with the Board's structure: its committees; term limits; orientation, advisory group usage, communication among Board, Executive Committee, & staff?
19. How well do Board members participate in organizational activities?
20. How involved is the Board in organizational fundraising?
21. What is the Board's involvement in strategic planning and/or identification of new areas of service?
22. What information, whether about BIG, nonprofit management or nonprofit boards, would help us to become more effective board members?
23. When you were elected to the board, did you have ideas on

how you would help the organization that has not happened?

The results were shared with the Board in a report dated March 2006 and presented for discussion at the April 2006 Board Meeting (during the Thursday evening Roundtable Discussions). The results were very revealing and a wide variety of answers were received. The report highlighted the percentages of each response, the percentage of each kind of response, and provided the narrative answers to each question.

The Board did not give itself enough time to thoroughly review each question and answer in depth. We did not collectively come to a consensus on what we should do next. The assessment was a good document. Unfortunately, we got caught up in crisis management and neglected this important governance aspect of a board for its improvement.

Chapter 20: Chairmen's Tribute to Youth Scholarships

I came up with the idea of establishing a scholarship program for BIG's members' children and grandchildren after getting an issue of National Active and Retired Federal Employees (NARFE). After reading that NARFE annually gave out sixty scholarships to their members' dependants, I noticed that none of the scholarship recipients were African-American. Scholarships and monetary awards for African American youth has always been a passion with me. When I was president of the Bay Area Urban Bankers Association, I had a similar experience. At the annual awards program for the Junior Achievement Program, everyone except African American students were receiving awards, so I approached the local Junior Achievement leadership with the idea of having an award for an outstanding African-American participant in the program and it was well-received. While the President of the Daly City Branch of the NAACP, I again was able to convince local school administrators on a $100.00 savings bond for an outstanding African-American student graduating from middle school to high school.

Prior to the 2003 National Training Conference, I worked with Richard Shields, the 2003 NTC Chair. The 2003 NTC was in Denver that year and we had a Chairman's Tribute to Youth luncheon and presented certificates of achievement to four students. However, the next year at the 2004 conference in Washington, D.C., I was able to obtain corporate contributions and during the luncheon gave out $4,500.00 in scholarships for students to attend college. At the 2005 NTC in Orlando, Florida, six students each received a $1,000.00 scholarship for their academic pursuit.

My daughter left home (the West Coast) in 1988 to attend Georgetown University and stayed afterwards to get her law degree at Catholic University. She is an attorney for a non-profit legal firm and one day agreed to do a fundraiser for me.

Her e-mail to me was very professional:

-----Original Message-----
From: Tracy C. McGhee
Sent: Thursday, February 23, 2006 9:07 AM
To: Chiles, Farrell J
Subject: fundraiser

Farrell:

To assist me in planning the fundraiser, please forward to me by mail a packet of BIG pamphlets, newsletters, write-ups, Farrell Chiles propaganda, or other useful items to market to potential sponsors, underwriters, etc. If these materials can be easily reproduced, please send at least 50 of each if available. Thank you.

Tracy

A later e-mail laid out her plans:

-----Original Message-----
From: Tracy C. McGhee
Sent: Wednesday, May 03, 2006 1:35 PM
To: Chiles, Farrell J
Subject: Fundraising Event

Dear Farrell:

Per your request, I have begun planning a fundraiser to raise funds for the BIG scholarship fund you have developed. My three friends, Sharon Brown, Devona Cole, and Connie Moore are on my committee. As you know, we have decided to do a Silent Auction. There will also be light refreshments and soft music during the event. It will be on Saturday, July 22, 2006 at American University in the School of International Studies Lounge from 6-10pm. We hope that you can attend this event to bolster it.

We are now in the process of trying to acquire sponsors and donors for the event. I am enclosing the Corporate Sponsorship letter and Donations Form for your review. If there is a problem with any language, please let me know. For uniformity and simplicity, I refer to the scholarship at all times as the Chairman's Youth Scholarship Fund ("CYSF"). I have opened up a designated bank account at Citibank to handle all monies associated with this event. Expenses will be paid from sponsorship dollars and donations. All remaining funds will go to BIG in one check within five business days of the close of the event. A full accounting will be provided at that time. If there are issues with this methodology, please let me know.

I will need a mailing list of who we should invite formally (BIG members, colleagues, etc.) Also, please forward the donation form to anyone you think might be willing to donate an auction item.

If this meets with your approval, I will proceed. I look forward to hearing from you.

Thank you.

Sincerely,
Tracy

The event was a success! I was in town for the NAACP annual convention and stayed over for the auction. Members from Region XI attended, plus friends and acquaintances of my daughter were all in attendance. The music was excellent, the food delicious, and the items for the auction hit the mark. The Silent Auction raised over $7,000. I was able to provide scholarships to students for the next two years until the proceeds and funds from other donations were depleted.

The Chairmen's Tribute to Youth or Chairmen's Youth Scholarship Fund was the forerunner of the BIG National Scholarship Program that was established in 2007. I had a role in that program as well. Providing scholarships to members' dependents is a membership benefit and an investment in the future – our youth.

Chapter 21: Rev. Dr. Benjamin Hooks

At noon on July 19, 2006, the FCC Benjamin Hooks Chapter of Blacks In Government honored Rev. Dr. Benjamin Hooks at the Federal Communications Commission (FCC) headquarters in the Commission Meeting Room. The event was spearheaded by Wesley Jarmon, the chapter president. All the current FCC Commissioners were in attendance and gave remarks. The room was filled with dignitaries. I had the opportunity to meet former Congressman Louis Stokes of Ohio, who was among the guests attending the event. Dr. Hooks was the first African-American appointed as a Commissioner at the FCC and served from 1972–1977 before succeeding Roy Wilkins as the Executive Director of the NAACP, who served in that position from 1977-1993.

The previous year in July 2005 at the NAACP's annual convention in Milwaukee, Wisconsin, I had the pleasure of assisting Dr. Hooks with the sale of his autobiography, "The March for Civil Rights: The Benjamin Hooks Story." He had a book signing and I controlled the line, collected the money, and had the buyers write their names on a small piece of paper to provide to Dr. Hooks for his autograph. I enjoyed working with him. At the end of the book signing, I of course got my autographed book which is now a part of my collection of biographies and autobiographies of African-American political and civil rights leaders.

I had briefly shared the stage with Dr. Hooks in Atlanta in 2002 at BIG's National Training Conference. I became an NAACP life member in June 1988, while Dr. Hooks was the Executive Director. My NAACP life membership plaque (bearing his signature) is proudly displayed in my home office next to my BIG life membership plaque.

Chapter 22: Behind the Scenes

Amendments to the Constitution: From 2002-2006, I authored every constitutional amendment submitted by the Los Angeles/Long Beach Area Chapter. In 2004, we submitted a record ten amendments. However, most were conforming amendments for others. We weren't successful at getting most of them passed. Most amendments are usually rejected by the Board's Constitution & Policy, Constitution Committee, by the Board, or by the Delegates Assembly. Two of our amendments did get approved.

National Resolutions: Each year the National Delegates Assembly considers resolutions submitted to the body for adoption. In 2005, I drafted a resolution pertaining to the Brown v. Board of Education and the minting of a coin in honor of the historic event in our Nation's history. I contacted Cynthia Davis, from Region VI, and asked her if she would submit it on behalf of her chapter. Cynthia went a step further and got the other two chapters in Arkansas to co-sponsor the resolution. During the Delegates Assembly, the resolution passed.

Monetary Assistance Program (MAP) Requests: MAP provides monetary assistance to chapters and regional councils to support their specific activities and projects that are in line with the goals and objectives of BIG. In this manner, BIG becomes more effective in accomplishing its goals and objectives.

Requests may be made for refundable or nonrefundable assistance.

- Monetary assistance that is not to be refunded may be awarded up to $1,500.
- Monetary assistance that is to be refunded must be repaid in 24 months. This amount may not exceed $3,000. Monetary assistance may range from $1,000 to $3,000.

- A combination of each type of assistance may be approved for a single program. This combination may not exceed $4,500.
- No more than one award of assistance may be made to a chapter or regional council within a three-year period.

As a member of the Los Angeles/Long Beach Area Chapter, I drafted two MAP requests. The first one was in 2001 for $4,500 ($1,500 nonrefundable) to support and finance the chapter's quarterly newsletter, "The BIG Connections". The chapter paid back the $3,000 within the agreeable 24 months. The second MAP for $1,500 (nonrefundable) was in 2004 to assist in the financing of the Brown v. Board of Education celebration.

STACK Request: This scholarship program facilitates training for career advancement and development opportunities for BIG's membership.

- The eligible applicant shall be a financial and active member of BIG for two consecutive years. The recipient must retain his/her financial status during the year in which the award is utilized.
- The scholarships are intended to underwrite specific training expenses associated with a specific government job or promotional opportunity. Applicants must document: (1) employer funds are not available for the training/education and (2) training desired as it relates to current or potential employment.
- The scholarship funds may be applied to tuition or associated costs including room and board, books, instructional or lab fees, travel to the training site or other documentable training related expense to an accredited institution only.

I encouraged a Los Angeles/Long Beach Area Chapter member to submit an application and she was approved for a STACK award in excess of $4,000.00.

Prestige Awards: The BIG National Prestige Awards Program is designed to give recognition to those members, chapters, and regions of Blacks In Government whose deeds and contribution in furtherance of the goals and objectives of the organization have been so exemplary and/or significant that they are deserving of special honor and praise. Similarly, the awards program recognizes individuals and organization outside of BIG for outstanding accomplishments.

- Meritorious Service Award - This honorary award provides the opportunity to recognize a BIG member for exemplary/outstanding contributions in the furtherance of BIG's goals and objectives.
- Distinguished Service Award - This honorary award provides the opportunity to recognize a BIG Chapter, Region or Group for exemplary/outstanding contributions in the furtherance of BIG's goals and objectives.
- Special Achievement Award - This honorary award provides the opportunity to recognize an individual or organization outside of BIG whose efforts and accomplishment have advanced African Americans progress in vital areas such as employment, education, civil rights, community and economic development and/or citizen participation.

I was pretty successful in assisting individuals and chapters in receiving these awards. I authored three Special Achievement Award nominations on behalf of the Los Angeles/Long Beach Area Chapter and two were winners – the Greater Los Angeles Federal Executive Board in 2001 and Nita Jones of AARP California in 2005. I was unsuccessful in 2006 when the Institute of Community Development (ICD) was nominated, but that organization lost to Navy Rear Admiral Charles Lilli, Commander of the Defense Supply Center Columbus (Ohio), who was well deserving of the award.

I was instrumental in writing and/or reviewing and editing, the nominations of four winners of the Meritorious Service Award – Mary

Carter in 2002; Kimberly Best-Tuten in 2003; Barbara Johnson Cox in 2005, and Deena Shepherd in 2007.

I authored the nomination for the Distinguished Service Award for the Los Angeles/Long Beach Area Chapter in 2004 and reviewed/edited the nomination for the New Kemet Harambe Chapter in 2006. Both chapters were winners of the award.

Presidential Appointments: I encouraged my second Executive Assistant Rebecca Lewis to apply for the National Protocol position. Kimberly Best-Tuten, my first Executive Assistant submitted her resume for National Membership Chair. Both were selected. When no one was selected for the Legal Review Committee Chair, I suggested to Ida Tyree-Hyche, my former speech writer and fellow Army Reserve warrant officer, that she apply for the open position. Ms. Tyree-Hyche had a Juris Doctorate from the Birmingham School of Law and I believed that she would make an outstanding contribution at the National level. Ida ended up serving in the position until she was deployed to Kuwait in support of Operation Iraqi Freedom. When the National Legislative Affairs position became vacant, I called Glen Smith, the former Region III Council President, and recommended that he apply for the position and he was appointed as Chair of the National Legislative Affairs Committee.

Chapter 23: Legal Cases

During my tenure as the Board Chair, Blacks In Government and the Board of Directors had our share of lawsuits. The Board spent a considerable amount of time in Executive Sessions reviewing, discussing, and making decisions on various law suits and legal issues that came before the Board. We were constantly being sued. When someone had a disagreement with a chapter and sued the chapter, they sued the National Organization, too. In most of the cases we prevailed. Some cases were arbitrated, others were settled, and some are still outstanding even as I write this book.

BIG maintains liability insurance and receives legal representation from the insurance company (depending on the type of case and whether they agree to represent us). We also maintained an outside counsel with Ronald C. Jessamy of the Law Offices of Ronald C. Jessamy, PLLC, in Washington, DC. Mr. Jessamy was representing BIG when I joined the Board and continued to do so throughout my tenure as Chair. Ron Jessamy is an outstanding attorney and represented BIG well. We had a super relationship. BIG probably wouldn't have gotten in some of the situations that we got in if we had consulted with him first and followed his advice when he gave it to us.

Prior to each Board meeting, Mr. Jessamy would send me a report on all the pending cases in which we were involved. I would have the report posted on the Board's BIGNET secured page for all Board members to review. On two occasions during my tenure, Mr. Jessamy came to a Board meeting and addressed the Board on the status of outstanding legal issues.

The case that we spent the most time on was Arthur J. Henderson, Jr. vs. Blacks In Government (BIG). This action arose because of an action by the National Executive Committee (NEC). Four members of the NEC brought charges against Mr. Henderson and the Board in accordance with the National Constitution and Robert Rules of Order conducted a hearing.

Article X of the BIG National Constitution is entitled, "Expulsion, Termination, or Removal". Section 4 (Complaints – National) states: (a) A complaint against a National Officer may be initiated by any three (3) National Officers. Upon receipt thereof, the Chair of the Board of Directors shall forward a copy of the complaint by registered mail to the Officer involved at the last address on file. Said Officer shall have fifteen (15) calendar days from date of receipt to answer in writing.

(b) The Board of Directors reserves the right to hear and act upon the charges and the Officer is entitled to a hearing before the Board of Directors if desired. The Officer may elect to have the decision made ex-parte on the basis of the complaint and the answer. The Board of Directors may appoint a special committee to hear the matter.

(c) The Board of Directors shall be the final level of appeal by either party of all complaints and grievances for which there has been final action.

The evening prior to the November 2001 Board meeting, the Board convened a special meeting to hear from the parties involved. After hearing both sides, the Board decided to remove Mr. Henderson as the National Secretary and restricted him from running for an elected office in BIG for 24 months.

Sometime later, Mr. Henderson made a request for copies of documents and files pertaining to his case. When he didn't receive them in a timely manner, he brought a lawsuit against BIG. The lawsuit, filed on August 21, 2002, sought relief and an injunction requiring BIG make certain documents available to him. In March 2003, a judge determined that Mr. Henderson was a member in good standing and that he had articulated a "proper purpose" for wanting access to the records. The judge entered a summary judgment in Mr. Henderson's favor. Mr. Henderson then filed a lawsuit for damages because he alleged that we did not provide due process in accordance with our constitution. He subsequently filed other lawsuits. Mr. Jessamy and I met with Mr. Henderson's attorney for a mediation conference as required in the rules of the Superior Court of the District of Columbia. We could not agree to resolve the case in arbitration. Eventually, we went to trial.

I attended the trial as the defendant (for BIG). Mr. Henderson testified along with two other witnesses for the Plaintiff. The defense (BIG), based on the testimonies of the plaintiff's witnesses, decided not to call any witnesses. I was available to testify along with Gerald Reed, the National President at the time of Mr. Henderson's removal.

On March 6, 2006, the Superior Court of the District of Columbia, Civil Division, ruled that the Plaintiff (Arthur Henderson) failed to meet his burden of proving his case by a preponderance of the evidence. The judge ordered and adjudged that the action be dismissed on the merits and that Blacks In Government recover our costs of the action. The plaintiff had 30 days to appeal the decision. He did not. The Arthur Henderson case was over. From the time that the Board removed Mr. Henderson as the National Secretary until the time the court dismissed the case was four years and four months. A lot of time and energy was expended. The Board had made a decision to stand by our original decision. Even though we did not always agree, we stayed strong as a Board. I was proud to be the Chair of the National Board of Directors of Blacks In Government.

Chapter 24: The BIG Family

It's great to be a part of the BIG family. I travel extensively and live out of hotels. It's nice to go to a city and have friends with whom I can fellowship with. The Board has a policy that whenever the Chair goes to a Region, the Board members of that region are notified.

I had a conference to attend in Chicago, Illinois and notified the Regional Directors and they immediately e-mailed the chapter presidents in the Chicago area of my trip. One evening, I had dinner with Eric Lee, President and members of the West Chicago United Chapter and the next day with Deena Sheppard, President of the New Kemet Harambe Chapter and one of her members.

While in Detroit visiting, on two different occasions, I had dinner with the Chapter President Sheila Sanders and New Detroit Chapter members. And when I was in Pine Bluff, Arkansas, Cynthia Davis, the National Secretary, arranged for dinner with several BIG members one evening, with a couple people driving over two hours to attend.

I was at a Combined Federal Campaign Regional Workshop in San Diego, California, and the Greater San Diego Chapter President, Horace Hill, invited me to join him and others for the San Diego Padres Opening Day baseball game. We enjoyed the game (it went into extra innings), enjoyed the beers, and the peanuts.

Prior to Hurricane Katrina, I was in New Orleans for a conference and was shown Nawlin's hospitality by Blanton Shepherd. At the time he was the Chapter President and he and two other local chapter presidents met at my hotel for drinks and conversation. Later in the week, other BIG members joined us for dinner at the Ruth's Chris Steak House. The dinner included city officials and a representative from the New Orleans Convention and Visitors Bureau. They sponsored the dinner. New Orleans was very much interested in hosting a National Training Conference. They didn't get the one they were bidding for that year. But eventually, they got the 2008 National Training Conference.

Spending time with my BIG family allowed me to get to know our membership better and them to know me. It was an opportunity I always looked forward to. Not only did I get out the hotel and see some of the city that I was visiting, I was able to meet members I had never met and talk to them in a small group (where I am at ease). We talked about BIG. I gave them my version of how we were as an organization - always accenting the positive.

I blew it once. I had to make a quick trip to Seattle. I was a speaker at a military conference. My plan was to fly to Seattle the evening before, make the speech in the morning, and leave in the early afternoon. Everything was going by the plan. I was walking in the hotel when I heard someone call my name. It was Charles Oliver, the Regional Director from Region X. Low and behold, Region X was having a Regional Council meeting in the same hotel that I was making the presentation. If I had made a courtesy call or sent an e-mail saying that I was coming to the area, I'm sure that I would have gotten a response and been informed of the Council meeting. I would have made changes to my flight arrangements. So, I learned my lesson. Regardless, of the length of time in a region, if I step on their soil, I should let the directors know.

Chapter 25: National Training Conference Site Selections

In September 2005, while attending the Congressional Black Caucus in Washington, D.C. I ran into Sheila Neal from the Detroit Convention and Visitors Bureau. I had met Sheila several years earlier, when Detroit first started in participating in the National Training Conference bidding. Sheila once flew out to Las Vegas where the Board was meeting to make a presentation to sell us on Detroit as the host city. On another occasion, the National Executive Committee was meeting in Detroit and Sheila arranged for a reception at the Charles Wright Museum of African American History and dinner at one of the casino hotels in an effort to show the benefits of selecting Detroit.

I grew up in Detroit. Most of my family (mother and siblings) still lives there. However, each year that Detroit bided for the NTC they lost. Sheila invited me to the Hyatt Hotel in D.C. for dinner and I met her there along with two of her associates from Detroit. We discussed Detroit's unsuccessful bids in the past and I shared with her what the successful cities presented that gave them the winning edge. I told her the process that the organization goes through to select a city for the NTC site. The NTC packages are quite competitive. BIG brings to a city at least 5,000 people (attendees, families, vendors, presenters, and others). We conduct ourselves in a professional manner. We shop and spend money in the host cities. Cities welcome our business. Each Convention and Visitors Bureau (CVB) that competes for our business is well aware of BIG and our NTC history. Each bureau is in the business of getting organizations to commit to their cities. It's a business. They all know each other. They all belong to the same professional organizations and attend the same annual conferences. They talk among themselves. As Chair, I allowed all the competing cities to attend our Thursday evening "Talk Around" and make presentations. I encouraged them to provide promotional premiums to the Board members to show their interest in obtaining our business.

However, each knew they were competing with others and that only one could win.

Once a region or city submits a bid, the packet goes to the Time & Place/Delegates Assembly Committee. The committee reviews the packets and reduces the competitors to the three finalists. They then contact the CVBs and arrange dates to visit the city for tours and presentations. They are wined and dined. The Time & Place/Delegates Assembly is one of the most sought after committee assignments. The committee uses a scoring system and the city with the top score gets their recommendation to the whole Board for approval.

Detroit made a bid for the 2013 National Training Conference. At our meeting in New York City in August 2006, the Board approved Detroit for the NTC site for 2013. You must be competitive. You must be persistent. Detroit became both and won the selection.

New Orleans was very similar. After winning the bid to host the 1999 NTC, which was very successful, they submitted three more times for future conferences. All were unsuccessful. They finally got the bid for 2008. However, they put together a very competitive packet and they never took rejection as the final answer, although they were not happy with our previous decisions to select other cities to host the NTC.

While I was on the Board, I believe that we improved the NTC site selection to ensure that all regions had an opportunity to bid and get a fair shake in the process. As a result, by the time I left the Board, every region (except Region X) had received an acceptance to host the NTC. Region X did not make a bid. We ensured that everyone knew the rules and the process. The Time & Place/Delegates Assembly Committee makes the recommendation to the Board and the Board approves or disapproves the recommendation. During my tenure on the Board, we always accepted the committee's recommendations. The decision upset some Board members, some regions, and some cities. In the end, the Board made the best decisions for Blacks In Government. That's what we were elected to do.

Chapter 26: Life Members

I have this thing about Life members. I've joined a lot of organizations. In most of them, I became a Life member. I do the math. If I 'm around for the next ten years, am I better off becoming a life member or a regular member (paying dues annually)? Usually, the answer is Life member. Currently, I am a regular member of two organizations. It's just not cost beneficial to become a life member.

With BIG, it's not an issue. With the cost of a life membership being only $300.00, paying for the life membership is by far a better deal.

I became obsessed with Life memberships and went on a mission to get the most Life members for the Los Angeles/Long Beach Area Chapter. My goal for 2001 – 2004 was to have each year the most Life members and to have the chapter's accomplishment listed in the National Training Conference's souvenir journal. I succeeded. Not only did the Los Angeles/Long Beach Area Chapter become the largest chapter in the organization with over 200 members, the chapter was the first to gain Platinum Elite Status with 108 Life members.

My team was able to get members to become Life members based on relationships and credibility. Over the years, I had developed a large rolodex of associates. Through my involvement with the Federal Executive Board, the Combined Federal Campaign, the Military, and community organizations, I had established myself as someone who was a professional and a person of integrity. When I went about asking people to become Life members, I was really banking on my relationship with them and their belief that I was a credible person.

Very seldom did I try to sell a Life Membership to someone I didn't know. That's a very difficult sell. However, I did sell Life memberships to others. But, they really sold themselves on the idea.

One Saturday, as the chapter president, I was presiding over a chapter meeting. I was the only one wearing a tie and blazer. One of the chapter members had invited her boss to the meeting. I believe that he was impressed with how I presented myself and how the members interacted at the meeting. So much so, he wrote a check for $300.00. No sell was necessary. No ask was needed. The gentleman wanted to be a part of something good. He was a city employee and it is generally difficult to recruit non-Federal workers. He was a professional and wanted to be a part of a professional organization. That's something else that I always emphasized. If you are an African American public service careerist, then you should belong to a professional organization. And, the premier organization for African-American government employees is Blacks In Government. During Public Service Recognition Week, I made sure that the new Life Member received a Public Service Recognition Award. As a matter of fact, the chapter gave out four such awards each year and the only way you could receive the award was to be a Life Member.

I admit acquiring Life members became quite an obsession. I would strongly suggest that prospective members join another chapter until they saved their money to become a Life member and then they could join our chapter. I was, in essence, selling Mercedes not Pintos. At our chapter meetings, during introductions, if you were a Life member, you were to state so – to embarrass any attendee who wasn't and to show your level of commitment to Blacks In Government.

Regardless of my tactics, the Los Angeles/Long Beach Area Chapter was able to become the largest chapter, have the most life members, and the most Gold Plus members in Blacks In Government. We were proud of our chapter and our accomplishments.

Chapter 27: Executive Assistants

Kimberly Best-Tuten was my first Executive Assistant. Her experience as a Public Affairs Officer complimented the Executive Assistant position. She was very professional in her demeanor and expected excellence from me. For the first two years that I was Chair, she also was my speech writer. Kimberly brought vision and her expertise in interpersonal skills to help me through some of the personality challenges within the organization. She later served for four years as the National Membership Chair and twice was the recipient of a BIG Presidential Award.

When Rebecca Lewis, my second Executive Assistant for two years, accepted the National Protocol position, I was in need for a new Executive Assistant. I called Barbara Johnson Cox and asked her to consider the position. Ms. Johnson Cox, the President of the Department of Labor Chapter, would end her presidency in March 2005 - after four years at the helm of one of the most productive and leading chapters in the organization.

In February 2005, I was in D.C. area for a meeting of another organization and I met with Ms. Johnson Cox for lunch at the Ritz Carlton Hotel in Crystal City, Virginia. We discussed the position and what it entailed. Ms. Johnson Cox was very enthusiastic about the prospect and challenge and agreed to accept the position. And, thus, I had my third Executive Assistant during my tenure as Board Chair.

I was immediately amazed at the professionalism and organizational skills that Ms. Johnson Cox exhibited and I knew that I had made the right decision. She requested a list of all the projects for the year in priority order and with their deadlines. She also took on the duties as speech writer. That meant drafting speeches for me to deliver at the National Delegates Assembly and at both the Opening and Closing Plenary Sessions. She maintained my daily schedule during the National Training Conference, coordinated meetings, ensured that I attended designated Agency Forums, and "covered my back", along with a multitude of other duties.

Ms. Johnson Cox had a critical eye and would politely inform me when something was wrong or when she disagreed with me and always made recommendations for improvement or correction. We became an outstanding team. I became a better Board Chair because of her.

Chapter 28: Working the Room / Networking

Susan RoAne, Keynote Speaker, is the bestselling author of "How to Work a Room ®" in 1988 and "The Secrets of Savvy Networking" in 1993. Her latest book, "Face to Face" was published in October 2008. I have the honor of my name and quotes appearing in all three books. I first met Susan in 1981 at a conference that I was attending. We stay in touch either by e-mail or by the occasional phone call. She has always been very supportive of me and my various activities and has served as a sounding board when I needed one.

From reading Susan's numerous books and applying their concepts, I have become very skillful at working a room and networking. Whenever I'm at a BIG event or any event, my role is to promote myself and BIG's image. Thus, I always do my best to approach people, ask them how their doing, thank them for all they do for BIG, and try to show that my leadership is a caring leadership.

At most National Training Conferences, especially the ones in Washington, D.C. where you have local commuters arriving at the hotel early, I usually get up early and walk the lobby, saying good morning and having light conversations. I enjoy meeting people. Hopefully, those early morning contacts left a favorable impression on a first time attendee or a BIG member that had not met a National leader of the organization. I felt my job as the Chair was to promote BIG at all times and sell the image that "BIG is a world-class organization. I am very comfortable meeting and talking to people one-on-one and in small groups. However, each year, what I dreaded the most was standing in front of over 3,000 people at the Opening Plenary Session and making a presentation. All I wanted to do was to get up, speak for less than eight minutes, and sit down. But I also had to represent the organization. Even though I read my speeches, I tried to deliver them in a professional manner that kept the audiences' interest. I was blessed to have three excellent speech writers during my five years as Chair. Each stressed the importance of rehearsing the speeches and delivering them with no errors. I had critics that always found something wrong, but after each speech, I received congratulations from quite a number of people and I was always asked for copies of my speeches from people in the audiences.

Blacks In Government allowed me to grow professionally with opportunities to speak and to meet leaders in the political environment and the public service sector. I had to hold conversations and talk about the issues of the day.

Before I leave for work every morning and when I'm at a hotel, the first thing I do when I wake up in the morning is to read the daily newspaper and catch CNN news. This exercise provides me with information on the latest news and gives me conversation points to use during the day. Reading is a natural for me. Reading the paper is a family tradition. I remember seeing my grandfather reading the paper at the breakfast table and I use to try to read the evening paper before my father, so that I could engage in the conversation about the front page articles and the sports section.

I believed that I had the advantage over others on the Board because of my "hidden" networking and "working the room" skills. I would strategically call them on the phone or send an e-mail just to say hello. I called that "reducing the space". Staying in touch with people is very important. These short e-mails and phone calls allowed me to continue to "sell" myself and my abilities as the Board Chair. They provided an opportunity to share ideas and sometimes they turned into "venting" sessions. But, each Board member knew me one-on-one. I tried to establish a positive relationship with each of them. I believe the approach worked. I was elected for a record five terms as the Board Chair.

Chapter 29: Board Chair – Bean Counter

At some point, I became known as the "bean counter". An old rule in politics is to do a poll before you run for the office. You gage where you are and where you need to go and then determine how to get there. To get elected Chair or Vice Chair of the Board, you need thirteen votes for the majority (if all Board members are voting). I also stressed to fellow Board members to get a motion passed requires a majority of thirteen votes. So if you communicate with the other Board members (prior to the introduction of the motion) regarding an issue, get a consensus, determine whether you have the support of thirteen others, then it's much easier to make the motion, have a person ready to second the motion and then have someone move to cut off debate, get the motion passed and move on. Unfortunately, most motions were made extemporaneously, with no coordination or communication, no buy-in from other members, and thus we had long discussions, amended motions, substitute motions, or motions to table.

As Chair and presiding officer of the board proceedings, I tried to give everyone the opportunity to speak on an issue – even more than the two times and two minutes that the standing rules allowed. If no Board member called me on the amount of time or the number of times that someone spoke, then it wasn't an issue to me. Sometimes, I overlooked someone who thought their time to speak came before the person that I had acknowledged, but that happened to everyone and thus cancelled out any dissatisfaction of not speaking at all. My job was to make sure no one was unhappy, because I needed their vote in the next election. I was always mindful of the next election and I always counted my votes. I counted them on a daily basis. Votes change just like the weather.

I had to learn to read the Board members. At any kind of meeting, people take on different roles. Over the years, identification has become easier. We had the dominators, the quiet ones, the intimidators and the conciliators, among others.

Chapter 30: Board of Directors

The National Board of Directors is comprised of twenty-five people. Twenty-two are regional directors. Each of the eleven regions is represented by two directors. The other three members of the Board are the National President, National Secretary, and National Treasurer.

Directors are elected for two year terms and term limits restrict them to elections of two terms or four consecutive years. There is a belief that Board members serve two masters – their region and the National Organization. I believe that once elected to the National Board, you serve in the best interest of the National Organization. That can be difficult, especially when you're elected by regional delegates and you have to report back to your region and chapters in the region. Regions expect you to represent their interests. Thus, being a Board member can be a balancing act.

Board members serve on the Regional Councils' Executive Committees as non-voting members. Even though some Board members also serve as chapter presidents, they are not allowed to represent their chapter as a regional delegate with a vote. They give written reports to their respective regions on actions of the Board and activities of the National Organization through reports received from the National President, Treasurer, and others. Board members also bring to the Board regional council items voted on by their regions, sign-off on by-laws, by-laws revisions, and introduce interest groups to the Board for chapter and charter approval. Board members also serve on Board committees.

Board members are elected at the National Delegates Assembly (NDA) by the registered delegates attending an annual assembly. The election of directors of each region is in alternate years. The number of the NDA varies from region to region and from year to year. In a small region, there may only be six delegates at the NDA and thus a candidate would only need four votes to get elected to the Board, whereas, in the largest region, Region, XI, there may be as many as 267 delegates, with a majority of 134 votes necessary for election.

Board members are the decision makers at the highest level of the organization. They have the duty to ensure that they exercise fiduciary responsibility and show due care and diligence in carrying out their responsibilities by representing the organization in a professional manner and making decisions in the best interest of the organization.

Board members assist their regions with chapter development, attend chapter and Regional Council meetings and events; assist in the resolution of chapter problems; provide guidance to regional council officers; and promote BIG within their respective regions. They give up their weekends for meetings, events, and to attend quarterly National Board meetings. That means plane travel, airport shuttles, staying in hotel rooms, early rises, long meetings, missed time with families, and in some cases, reporting to work on a Monday morning without having anytime off during the weekend. It means getting job work done late in the evening or early morning, checking e-mails and phone calls, and staying in touch with love ones. It means missing church on some Sunday mornings, juggling schedules, skipping other meetings and events; and making necessary sacrifices for Blacks In Government. Did I miss anything?

Chapter 31: Board Chair Elections

Each year, I was very cognizant of the Board's composition and whether the changes on the Board would affect my chances of re-election. When I joined the Board in 2001 there were eight female Board members. The trend over the next five years that I ran for the Board Chair position showed an increase in the number of female Board members. In 2002 there were 10; 2003 – 11; 2004 – 13; 2005 – 13; and 2006 – 15. I was keenly aware of the numbers and kept my fingers crossed that there wasn't an uprising or an attempt to exert "Women Power". I would have abdicated. I did not want to get defeated – not by anyone. I felt the best chance for anyone to defeat me was Angela Thorpe-Harris. Thus, I always encouraged her to run for Vice Chair and gave her my support each time she ran. I also gave female members the majority of the Board committee chair positions. One year, while running for re-election, I had Tonya Davis, a member of my Los Angeles/Long Beach Area Chapter and a Mary Kay consultant, design a nice private spa collection of four fragrances, wrapped in a thin gold sheer material and tied with a thin black ribbon with the words "Re-Elect Farrell Chiles". Every female member received the cache two weeks prior to the election. Another year, I mailed each female Board member an advanced copy of the book published by the National Council of Negro Women entitled, "Tomorrow Begins Today: African American Women as We Age". I got Dr. Dorothy Height to autograph the books to each one personally. I was going for the knock-out punch. I needed the female vote.

In late 2001, in preparation for the Board election in January 2002, I came up with a model strategy that would eventually work well in all my election campaigns. My goal was to win on the first ballot. To accomplish this goal, my strategy was to (1) sweep four regions – eight votes; (2) split four regions – four votes; (3) get 50% of the female vote; and (4) get 100% of the Board's Executive Committee members – three votes. Total votes – 15. My fallback goal was to get 13 votes. If there were too many running for the Chair position and I thought there might be a run-off, my goal was to obtain 8 to 9 votes and work to ensure that no opponent received more votes than me (on the first ballot).

In the 2002 election, I received 52.2% of the votes. In 2003, in a run-off election, I won with 60.0% of the votes. In 2001, my first year on the Board, Ellen Dyson defeated her opponent by gaining 72.0% of the votes. I always wanted to top that percentage and in 2004, I received 72.7% of the votes. I then set a goal of 75%. However, in the election of 2005, I had two opponents. I won on the first ballot, but only obtained 60.0% of the votes. Finally, in 2006, I was unopposed for re-election and thus by acclamation I received 100% of the votes.

After each Delegates Assembly, I would send all the Board members and Executive Committee members who were elected or re-elected a congratulation card. While the election results were being announced, I was writing a personal note on each congratulatory card and addressing the envelopes. I would then have my Executive Assistant deliver them to the hotel front desk for pick-up with a message that they had an envelope waiting for them. I also got different vendors, corporate sponsors, and convention & visitor bureaus to provide gifts for my Board members. Each year, I would send every Board member and the Executive Committee members Kwanzaa cards for them to receive by December 26th. I would send each an e-mail asking for their support and vote. And I would call some and ask for their votes and for others, I would have key communicators call them and ask them to vote for me or let me know if they were for me or not. I stayed on top of the potential votes. I had a listing of all the Board members with three columns – "Yes", "Maybe", and "No". In 2002, I purchased 24 post card size prints from the store Successories with themes such as Leadership, Confidence, Integrity, etc. I was to purchase 24 of the same cards, but I let the saleslady talk me into buying a variety of them. That was a major problem. I had to decide who would get which ones. I also went to BIG Lots and found 24 nice frames for the cards. The cards, framed looked very impressive. One year, Priscilla Martin, a Los Angeles/Long Beach Area Chapter member, provided me with pens with laser lights to give to the Board Members. The pens had written on them "Vote for Farrell Chiles".

I took winning very seriously. I take leadership very seriously. I aspired to the leadership of the Board because I felt that the Board Chair position provided me the best opportunity to make the greatest difference and move the organization forward.

Chapter 32: National Constitution and the Board of Directors

Article VIII, Section 1, D, (2) of the National Constitution states, "To be eligible for any National Office, an individual must have been a regular member in good standing for at least three (3) years and have held an elected office at either of the Chapter, Regional, or National level for at least one (1) term.

Fortunately, for me, this section was newly amended at the Delegates Assembly in 2002 to read as it is currently written, When I was elected to the National Board of Directors in August 2000, I had been a member for only two years and five months. I started my term as President of the Los Angeles/Long Beach Area Chapter in January 2000 and thus had served in the position for only seven and a half months (not at least one term).

At the Delegates Assembly in 2000, another amendment to the National Constitution created term limits. Article VIII, Section 1, C, (2) was amended to read, "Regional Directors shall serve no more than two (2) two-year terms or four consecutive years. However, they shall be eligible for election to all other offices". Since I was elected to the Board, prior to the effective date of the amendment, I became "grandfathered" with all the other Board members and the count for the term limit requirement started January 2001. Thus, I was eligible to serve six years on the Board.

During my tenure on the Board, I served with a total of 52 other Board members, to include four former Chairs, three future Chairs, three National Presidents, and one future National President.

Chapter 33: A Legacy of Leadership

Sometime around the first of June 2006, I decided to act on an idea that I came up with in 2004. I wanted to provide a report to the BIG membership on the Chairs of the National Board of Directors. BIG is always promoting past presidents, but I wanted to highlight the past Chairs of the Board. So, my Executive Assistant, Barbara Johnson Cox, and I embarked upon a project to identify and contact each previous Board Chair for current photos, bios, and leadership statements to include in a pamphlet. Some of the earlier Chairs were no longer active in the organization and it took some efforts to contact them. We found one by searching the internet and another one was located by an associate of mine who had access to certain records. We were finally able to get the information and assembled the presentation in a nice colored pamphlet. We had 800 copies printed and provided copies to the National Delegates Assembly Team for inclusion in the delegates' bags. The pamphlet was a success. Members received a piece of BIG's history that was never presented before in this fashion. Later, the pamphlet was shared with others via the BIGNET. Due to the lack of funds, we were unable to provide each BIG member a copy of the report. For those that received a copy, they have a unique historical document that shares the legacy of BIG's leadership, the men and women who attained the highest position in BIG, and their remarkable stories of success.

Epilogue

"Next to the assumption of power is the responsibility of relinquishing it" – Benjamin Disraeli

On December 28, 2006 as I was ending my third two-year term on the Board and my last year as Board Chair, I requested that Leonard Stone to send an e-mail to the BIG membership on my behalf via BIGNET.

From: Leonard T. Stone Sent: Thursday, December 28, 2006 11:41 AM
To: leonard.stone@wpafb.af.mil
Subject: To BIG Membership from the National Chairman of the Board - Farrell J. Chiles
Importance: High

Greetings BIG Members:

As I end my tenure as the Chair of the National Board of Directors, I thank you for your allegiance to BIG. I have stated both publicly and privately my admiration and high regards for your commitment and dedication to BIG. BIG can only survive if we believe in it, work for it, and dedicate ourselves to it.

I am sincerely grateful for the trust and support you gave me during my five years as Chairman - it has been a rewarding experience which has brought me many new friendships. I am indebted to the National Board of Directors for their confidence, encouragement, and challenge over the years. I thank the National Executive Committee for its leadership achievements. I salute each of you for your enterprise and unselfishness.

BIG is a great organization which has attained a position of prestige, respect, and influence, through times of turbulence and change, struggle and excitement-and stands as a monument to those who envisioned it. As we face another future, another cycle, another dawn, let us never forget that - **"As long as there is government - there will be - Blacks In Government!"**

Continue to embrace the principles of equity, excellence, and opportunity. It has been an honor and privilege to serve you.

Farrell J. Chiles
Chairman of the Board
National Board of Directors

==

Thank You For Thinking BIG!

Blacks In Government®

BIOGRAPHICAL INFORMATION

FARRELL J. CHILES
CHAIRMAN OF THE BOARD
BLACKS IN GOVERNMENT

Mr. Farrell J. Chiles serves as Chief, Human Resources Division, 63rd Regional Readiness Command (RRC), in Los Alamitos, California.

Mr. Chiles began his federal government career in 1992 with the United States Army Reserve's 300th Military Police Command, Inkster, Michigan, as a Military Personnel Specialist. In 1993, he accepted a Management Analyst position with the West Los Angeles Veterans Administration Hospital. In 1996, he became the Chief of the Special Actions Branch at the 63d Regional Readiness Command until he was promoted to his current position.

Mr. Chiles joined Blacks In Government in March 1998 and became the President of the Los Angeles/Long Beach Area Chapter of Blacks In Government in January 2000. In January 2001, he joined Blacks In Government's National Board of Directors representing Region IX. He was elected Chairman of the Board in January 2002 and re-elected as Chairman in 2003, 2004, and 2005. On January 20, 2006, he was re-elected as Chairman for a record fifth consecutive year.

Mr. Chiles received his Bachelor of Science degree in Political Science from the University of the State of New York. He is a graduate of the Greater Los Angeles Federal Executive Board's Leadership Associates Program. Also, he has completed the Organizational Leadership for Executives Program and the Personnel Management for Executives Course.

He is a Life member (Gold Plus) of Blacks In Government, the NAACP, the Veterans of Foreign Wars, ROCKS, Inc. and many other organizations. He is a Vietnam Veteran and a chief warrant officer in the United States Army Reserves with over 35years of service to his country. In 2004, he was mobilized for one year in support of Operation Enduring Freedom.

He, Mr. Chiles, epitomizes the qualities of an outstanding leader: commitment, honor, and perseverance. He strives to make a positive difference for others by his involvement with professional and community affiliations. He currently serves on the board of directors of the Christian Service Charities and the Orange County Combined Federal Campaign Local Federal Coordinating Committee.

Appendix A: Milestones

March 1998	Joined BIG as a Life Member (West Los Angeles VAMC Chapter)
August 1998	Attended NTC in Wash, D.C. and received Life Membership Plaque
August 1999	Attended NTC in New Orleans, LA (featured in the BIG Reporter)
October 1999	Nominated to run for President of the Region IX Council (lost)
November 1999	Joined the Los Angeles/Long Beach Area Chapter
December 1999	Elected President of the Los Angeles/Long Beach Area Chapter
August 2000	Elected to represent Region IX on the National Board of Directors (2001-2002)
December 2000	Resigned as President of the Los Angeles/Long Beach Area Chapter
January 2001	Sworn in as a member of the National Board of Directors
January 2002	Elected Chair of the National Board of Directors
August 2002	Re-elected to the National Board of Directors (2003-2004)

January 2003	Re-elected Chair of the National Board of Directors
January 2004	Re-elected Chair of the National Board of Directors
August 2004	Re-elected to the National Board of Directors (2005-2006)
January 2005	Re-elected Chair of the National Board of Directors
January 2006	Unanimously re-elected Chair of the National Board of Directors (record 5th consecutive year)
December 31, 2006	Leaves National Board of Directors (due to constitutional term limit requirement)

Appendix B: CONGRESSIONAL RECORD

BLACK HISTORY MONTH -- (Extensions of Remarks - February 06, 2007)

SPEECH OF

HON. JUANITA MILLENDER-McDONALD

OF CALIFORNIA

IN THE HOUSE OF REPRESENTATIVES

TUESDAY, FEBRUARY 6, 2007

- Ms. MILLENDER-M**CDONALD**. Madam Speaker, during the month of February, we celebrate Black History Month. This year's theme is "From Slavery to Freedom: The Story of Africans in the Americas."

- I would like to call the attention of my colleagues to a man who exemplifies the characteristics of a leader in the African American community. It is with great pride that I introduce and honor Farrell J. Chiles as he celebrates his 9th year as a member of Blacks In Government (BIG) and on completion of his 5th consecutive year as its Chairman of the Board.

- In 2000, Mr. Chiles began his leadership role within BIG as the President of the Los Angeles/Long Beach Area Chapter. The following year, he was elected to the board of directors of the National Organization.

- In 2002, Mr. Chiles became the Chairman of the Board and has been re-elected for 4 consecutive years. During his chairmanship, the organization has grown and achieved remarkable successes.

- Mr. Chiles is also a Life Member of the NAACP and the ROCKS, Inc., and an associate member of the Tuskegee Airmen, Inc.

- Mr. Chiles is presently employed with the Department of the Army, at the 63rd Regional Readiness Command in Los Alamitos, California where he serves as the Division Chief of the Human Resources Division. He is a member of the United States Army Reserve, a Vietnam Veteran, and was mobilized for a year in support of Operation Enduring Freedom.

- He is a Life member and former board member of the United States Army Warrant Officers Association. Mr. Chiles is also a Life Member of the Reserve Officers Association. During Black History Month in 2005, he presented a report at its Mid-Winter Conference entitled "African American Warrant Officers--In Service to their Country--Their History, Achievement, and Contributions to the Military and the United States." This year, his presentation is on African American Warrant Officers during World War II.

- Mr. Chiles served on the 37th Congressional District's Veterans Congressional Council and is a Life Member of the Veterans of Foreign Wars.

- It is my sincere hope that my colleagues will join me in honoring and recognizing Mr. Chiles and his significant accomplishments throughout his career, his leadership with Blacks In Government, and his service to the African American community and his country.

  END

Appendix C: BIG Election Results - Top 20 Winning Margins (2000-2006)

2006	
Board Chair	
Farrell J. Chiles	100.0% (uncontested)
2003	
Region XI - Board of Directors	
Darlene Young	87.5%
Dione Bowlding	12.5%
2006	
Assistant Treasurer	
Norma Samuel	86.2%
Chris K. Sese-Khalid Sr.	13.8%
2000	
National President	
Gerald Reed	78.6%
Oscar Eason	21.4%
2006	
Region X - Board of Directors	
Harrison McMillan Jr.	75.7%
Remond Henderson	24.3%
2006	
National President	
Darlene Young	75.5%
Matthew Fogg	19.4%
Remond Henderson	5.1%

2003
Executive Vice-President

Charlene Lee	74.3%
Larry Harris	15.2%
Ralph Browne, Jr.	10.6%

2004
Board Chair

Farrell J. Chiles	72.7%
Remond Henderson	27.3%

2002
Region VIII - Board of Directors

Greta Jones-Sanders	72.7%
Deborah Dawkins	27.3%

2002
3rd Vice President

Karen Griffin	72.4%
Charlie Hampton	27.6%

2006
Region VI - Board of Directors

Duane Braxton	72.4%
Shelly Warren	27.6%

2001
Board Chair

Ellen Dyson	72.0%
Julius Crouch	28.0%

2005
Region X - Board of Directors

Lilyian Caswell-Isley	72.0%
Oscar Eason	28.0%

2002	
Region IV - Board of Directors	
Doris Sartor	71.1%
Danny Thomas	28.9%

2000	
Region XI - Board of Directors	
Farrell J. Chiles	69.7%
Donna Thomason	30.3%

2001	
Executive Vice-President	
Gregg Reeves	68.7%
Larry Harris	31.3%

2005	
Region XI - Board of Directors	
J. David Reeves	67.3%
Jacque Ballard	32.7%

2006	
First Vice-President	
J. David Reeves	66.8%
Matthew Fogg	26.3%
Janice Hall	6.9%

2005	
Region VIII - Board of Directors	
Gary Blackmon	65.0%
Deborah Dawkins	35.0%

2002	
Region XI - Board of Directors	
J. David Reeves	64.1%
Joyce Glover	35.9%

Appendix D: Blacks In Government's National Election Results (2000 – 2006)

2000

President		
Gerald Reed	372	78.6%
Oscar Eason	102	21.4%
1st Vice-President		
Margaret Stephens	288	61.0%
Matthew Fogg	181	39.0%
3rd Vice-President		
Karen Griffin	259	56.0%
Larry Harris	202	44.0%
Secretary		
Arthur Henderson	254	54.0%
Edna Harvey Battle	216	46.0%
Region IX Director		
Farrell Chiles	23	69.7%
Donna Thomason	10	30.3%

2001

Executive Vice-President		
Gregg Reeves	347	68.7%
Larry Harris	158	31.3%
2nd Vice-President		
Charlene Lee	461	100%

Corresponding Secretary		
Dawn Lawson	469	100%
Treasurer		
Abe Joseph	469	100%

2002

President		
Rawle King	77	10.9%
J. David Reeves	199	32.3%
Gregg Reeves	216	35.0%
Oscar Eason	50	8.1%
Larry Harris	18	2.9%
Howard Ervin	57	9.2%
President Run-off		
J. David Reeves	250	42.1%
Gregg Reeves	345	57.9%
1st Vice-President		
Margaret Stephens	342	56.6%
Matthew Fogg	263	43.4%
3rd Vice-President		
Karen Griffin	429	72.4%
Charlie Hampton	169	27.6%
Secretary		
Dawn Lawson	576	100%
Assistant Treasurer		
Faye Stewart-Henderson	310	50.1%
Sylvia Johnson-Herring	293	49.9%

Region I		
Dan Corria	13	100%
Region II		
Merton Simpson	24	100%
Region III		
Johnita Pitts	16	51.6%
Glenn Smith	9	29.0%
Lisa Dixon	6	19.4%
Region IV		
Danny Thomas	22	28.9%
Doris Sartor	54	71.1%
Region V		
Oscar Williams	29	59.2%
David Groves	20	40.8%
Region VI		
Katherine Cage	44	100%
Region VII		
David Hampton	27	100%
Region VIII		
Greta Jones-Sanders	8	72.7%
Debra Dawkins	3	27.3%
Region IX		
Farrell J. Chiles	44	100%
Region X		
Charles Oliver	11	61.1%
Opponent	7	38.9%

Region XI		
J. David Reeves	172	64.1%
Joyce Glover	95	35.9%

2003

Executive Vice President		
Charlene Lee	387	74.3%
Larry Harris	79	15.2%
Ralph Browne	55	10.6%
2nd Vice President		
Rawle King	211	40.5%
Walt Washington	178	34.2%
Danny Thomas	132	25.3%
Run-off		
Walt Washington	279	53.8%
Rawle King	240	46.2%
Treasurer		
Abe Joseph	479	100%
Corresponding Secretary		
Angela Harvey	279	53.9%
Constance Braxton	239	46.1%
Region I		
Ralph Browne, Jr.	6	100%
Region II		
Alma Garlington	20	100%
Region III		
Regina Kennedy	12	42.9%

Cheryl Keitt	10	35.7%
Lisa Dixon	6	21.4%
Run-off		
Regina Kennedy	17	60.7%
Cheryl Keitt	11	39.3%
Region IV		
C. Jacquie Beatty	56	100%
Region V		
Ellen Dyson	30	100%
Region VI		
Angela Thorpe-Harris	10	61.3%
Alfred Hunt	12	38.7%
Region VII		
Delores Ivy	24	100%
Region VIII		
Richard Shields	9	60.0%
Debra Dawkins	6	40.0%
Region IX		
J.B. Larkins	39	100%
Region X		
Remond Henderson	27	100%
Region XI		
Darlene Young	196	85.5%
Dione Bowlding	28	12.5%

2004

Gregg Reeves	208	39.8%
Darlene Young	314	60.2%
1st Vice President		
Matthew Fogg	291	56.5%
Karen Griffin	224	43.5%
3rd Vice President		
Richard Shields	290	58.0%
Wesley Jarmon	210	42.0%
National Secretary		
Cynthia Davis	499	100%
Assistant Treasurer		
Faye Stewart-Henderson	493	100%
Region I		
Dan Corria	6	100%
Region II		
Joyce Jones	9	50.0%
Barbara Johnson	6	33.3%
Merton Simpson	3	16.7%
Run-off		
Joyce Jones	11	61.1%
Barbara Johnson	7	38.9%
Region III		
Jackie Pitts	23	100%

Region IV		
Dr. Doris Sartor	71	100%
Region V		
Oscar Williams	44	100%
Region VI		
Katherine Cage	31	100%
Region VII		
David Hampton	21	100%
Region VIII		
Gary Blackmon	13	65.0%
Debra Dawkins	7	35.0%
Region IX		
Farrell J. Chiles	29	60.4%
Kenneth Pearson	16	33.3%
Earl Bryers	3	6.3%
Region X		
Charles Oliver	16	55.2%
Opponent	13	44.8%
Region XI		
J. David Reeves	99	48.3%
Jacque Ballard	65	31.7%
Shirley Harrington-Watson	42	20.0%
Run-off		
J. David Reeves	132	67.3%
Jacque Ballard	64	32.7%

2005

Executive Vice President		
Doris Sartor	237	48.3%
Charlene Lee	234	47.6%
John Lyons	20	4.1%
Run-off		
Doris Sartor	262	52.6%
Charlene Lee	236	47.4%
2nd Vice President		
Walt Washington	269	55.9%
Richard Shields	212	44.1%
Treasurer		
Faye Stewart-Henderson	446	100%
Corresponding Secretary		
Janice Hall	192	39.6%
Contress Braxton	187	38.2%
Edna White	105	22.2%
Run-off		
Contress Braxton	251	51.1%
Janice Hall	240	48.9%
Region I		
Palmer Doiley	5	100%
Region II		
Alter Cochran	14	100%
Region III		
Regina Kennedy	17	100%

Region IV		
Mary Peoples	41	63.0%
Anthony Rhodes	24	37.0%
Region V		
Lillian Barnett	24	54.5%
David Groves	20	45.5%
Region VI		
Angela Thorpe-Harris	25	100%
Region VII		
Delores Ivy	21	100%
Region VIII		
Debra Dawkins	12	54.5%
Genola Smith	10	45.5%
Region IX		
Toni Martin	37	100%
Region X		
Lilyian Caswell-Isley	10	41.6%
Oscar Eason	7	29.2%
Charlie Hampton	7	29.2%
2nd Run-off		
Lilyian Caswell-Isley	18	72.0%
Oscar Eason	7	28.0%
Region XI		
Gerald Reed	213	100%

2006

President		
Darlene Young	386	75.5%
Matthew Fogg	99	19.4%
Remond Henderson	26	5.1%
1st Vice President		
J. David Reeves	338	66.8%
Matthew Fogg	133	26.3%
Janice Hall	35	6.9%
3rd Vice President		
Richard Shields	156	31.1%
Beverly Johnson	198	39.4%
Charlie Hampton	148	29.5%
Run-off		
Richard Shields	306	60.6%
Beverly Johnson	199	39.4%
National Secretary		
Cynthia Davis	236	46.9%
Bobbie Bingham-Morrow	113	22.5%
Yolanda Brown-Harris	92	18.3%
Lorraine Townsend	62	12.3%
Run-off		
Cynthia Davis	316	62.8%
Bobbie Bingham-Morrow	187	37.2%
Assistant Treasurer		
Norma Samuel	430	86.2%
Chris K. Sese-Kahlis Sr.	69	13.8%

Region I		
Elijah Drew	16	100%
Region II		
Joyce Jones	24	100%
Region III		
Lois Miles	12	57.1%
Beatrice Gallatin	9	42.9%
Region IV		
Anthony Rhoades	30	56.6%
Gwen Buffington	16	30.2%
Tony Webster	7	13.2%
Region V		
Charlene Lee	45	100%
Region VI		
Duane Braxton	21	72.4%
Shelley Warren	8	27.6%
Region VII		
Melvin Davis	15	100%
Region VIII		
Gary Blackmon	14	100%
Region IX		
Kenneth Pearson	21	61.8%
J.B. Larkins	13	38.2%
Region X		
Harrison McMillan	28	75.7%
Remond Henderson	9	24.3%

Region XI		
Jacque Ballard	130	61.3%
Wesley Jarmon	82	38.7%

National Election Results (2001 – 2006)

2001

Delegates elected Gregg Reeves as the Executive Vice-President. He won against Larry Harris with 347 votes equating to 68.7% of the vote. Charlene Lee was unopposed for Second Vice-President. Dawn Lawson for Corresponding Secretary and Abe Joseph for National Treasurer did not receive any opposition.

Eight incumbents from the Board of Directors were re-elected. All eight were unopposed. The three new members were elected for 2002 were Cheryl Keitt (Region III), Remond Henderson (Region X) – he termed out as National Treasurer, and Darlene Young (Region XI).

2002

Six excellent candidates ran for National President in 2002: Howard Ervin, Region VI; Larry Harris, Region XI; Gregg Reeves, Region VI; Oscar Eason, Region X; Rawle King, Region XI; and J. David Reeves, Region XI. Neither candidate received over 50% of the vote on the first ballot. In a run-off between Gregg Reeves and J. David Reeves, Gregg Reeves won 345-250 capturing 57.9% of the vote.

Margaret Stephens was re-elected First Vice-President; Karen Griffin, Third Vice- President; Dawn Lawson, National Secretary; and in a closely contested race, Faye Steward-Henderson defeated Sylvia Johnson-Herring 310-293 capturing 51.3% of the vote.

Seven members of the Board of Directors were re-elected; one incumbent was defeated and three incumbents did not run for re-election. Four incumbents ran unopposed and one new candidate had no opposition. Of the three incumbents that faced opposition, they received 59.2%, 72.7% and 64.1% of the votes. The four new Board members for 2003 were Jackie Pitts (Region III); Dr. Doris Sartor (Region IV); Katherine Cage (Region VI), and Charles Oliver (Region X).

2003

In the 2003 election for Executive Vice-President, Charlene Lee won on the first ballot with 387 votes representing 74.3% of the votes.

Her opponents were Larry Harris and Ralph Browne, Jr. Walter Washington from Region X won in a run-off with Rawle King from Region XI for 2nd Vice-President. Also elected were Abe Joseph, Jr., Treasurer and Angela Harvey, Corresponding Secretary

Eight incumbents from the Board of Directors were re-elected. Six incumbents ran unopposed; one incumbent was defeated; two incumbents defeated challenges; two decided not to run for re-election; and one new candidate was not opposed. The three new board members elected for 2004 were Regina Kennedy, Region III; Angela Thorpe-Harris, Region VI; and Delores Ivy, Region VII.

2004

Darlene Young was elected President winning with 314 votes or 60.2%. I dubbed the election as the "Metro Race". I believe that many Region XI delegates took the Metro to vote and then returned to work. Darlene Young had an advantage that the election was held in Washington, D.C., in Region XI, and she was very popular.

Matthew Fogg was elected 1st Vice-President and Richard Shields was elected as 3rd Vice President. Cynthia Davis and Faye Stewart-Henderson, both from Region VI, were re-elected National Secretary and Assistant Treasurer, respectively.

Ten incumbents from the Board of Directors were re-elected. Five incumbents ran unopposed; one incumbent was defeated; four incumbents defeated challenges; and one decided not to run for re-election Interesting, Jackie Pitts, the incumbent from Region III, had a person nominated to run against her, however she received all the votes. The other two opposed incumbents were me and J. David Reeves. We both had two opponents. I won on the first ballot with 60.4% of the votes and J. David Reeves won in a run-off with 67.3% of the votes. The two new board members elected for 2005 were Joyce Jones, Region II and Gary Blackmon, Region VIII.

2005

Dr. Doris Sartor won the race for Executive Vice-President in a run-off against Charlene Lee. Dr. Sartor gained 52.6% of the votes. Walter Washington, 2nd Vice- President, was re-elected and Faye Stewart-Henderson was unopposed for Treasurer. Contress Braxton won in a run-off for Corresponding Secretary.

Several Board members were ineligible for re-election due to term limits and we had a record number of people voted on the board. Four incumbents were unopposed and re-elected; three new candidates were unopposed; and four new candidates won in contested races. The seven new Board members for 2006 were Palmer Doiley, Region I; Alter Cochran, Region II; Mary Peoples, Region IV; Lillian Barnett, Region V; Deborah Dawkins, Region VIII; Toni Martin, Region IX; and Lilyian Caswell-Isley, Region X.

2006

Darlene Young was re-elected President with 75.5% of the votes. J. David Reeves won the 1st Vice-President position with 66.8% of the votes. Richard Shields, in a run-off, was re-elected as 3rd Vice-President. Cynthia Davis won re-election as National Secretary after defeating an opponent in a run-off. Norma Samuel was elected as Assistant Treasurer.

In the elections for the National Board of Directors, eight Board members were termed out (including me); three incumbents ran unopposed; one incumbent defeated two challengers; and two new candidates ran unopposed. The eight new Board members for 2007 were Elijah Drew, Region I; Lois Miles, Region III; Charlene Lee, Region V; Duane Braxton, Region VI; Melvin Davis, Region VII; Kenneth Pearson, Region IX; Harrison McMillan, Region X; and Jacque Ballard, Region XI.

Appendix E: 2004 Annual Corporate Report – Message from the Chairman of the Board

A Proud Past… A Bright Future.

Blacks In Government (BIG) proves once again that an organization that pursues the right strategy and acts decisively can be successful even in an incredibly challenging economic environment. Without a doubt, 2004 was a challenging and exciting year for BIG. We faced many challenges, but the strength of our enterprise, the resilience of our operations, and the dedication and expertise of our populace saw us through another successful year. The ability to respond quickly and effectively has always set BIG apart, and this year was no exception.

On behalf of the National Board of Directors, I am pleased to report that 2004 was a year of solid achievement. We have developed a rigorous approach to sustainability, with a long-term plan for excellence. We took steps that strengthened the global leadership of our enterprise. More importantly, we made a number of strategic moves designed to build enduring member value and positioned our organization for strong growth by developing new strides in our internal operational efficiency, and enhanced our solid financial position by reducing spending and maintaining strategic investments.

Our past successes are the foundation for future excellence. We continue to build on long-term strategies, as embodied in our policies, to reflect the changing needs of our organization and a greater ability to deliver results to you, our members. Some of our key accomplishments include the following:

The human rights of our members are of paramount importance. BIG publicly announced its support for the Civil Rights Act, also known as the Fairness Act of 2004. In 2004, BIG participated in the NAACP Federal Sector Task Force Summit IV as well as the National Coalition for Equity in Public Service First Diversity Summit, both held in

Washington, D.C. In addition, BIG hosted its Second Discrimination and Disparate Treatment of Government Workers Summit which focused on solutions to the problem of discrimination in the workplace in Washington, DC.

Education is our primary focus, as we continue to foster career development. In an effort to help improve BIG's services and programs, the "New Epinion Survey" was posted on BIGNET soliciting member viewpoint. In 2004, BIG launched several successful Officer Leadership Training sessions designed to accelerate member leadership skills; during the 26th Annual National Training Conference (NTC), BIG presented its initial partnership with the U.S. Department of Agriculture Graduate School, the Office of Personnel Management, Georgetown University, the University of Phoenix, the DeVry University and Trinity College; in addition, BIG held its first Senior Executive Service Boot Camp. Partnerships implemented in 2004, also included the value added Federal Deposit Insurance Corporation (FDIC) Money Smart Training Program

BIG has long enjoyed a reputation as a leader when it comes to "corporate" commitment to its members. As you will see in the pages that follow our organization has a sharpened strategy and ambitious objectives.

In the year ahead, we will face continued challenges, such as economic uncertainty, but we are well positioned to meet these challenges and opportunities. We are more innovative in our business approach; we are unrelenting in our efforts to lower expenses through the quality process. We will also pursue leading-edge technology development to uncover the breakthroughs that our members will need to meet the challenges of the future.

It is our hope that this report will not only convey to you the great efforts we are making, and the progress already made, but also our conviction that we still have a long way to go. Despite facing many challenges, BIG executed with discipline and indications for the year ahead are very encouraging.

Appendix F: 2005 Installation of Officers

Department of State
Washington, D.C.
January 25, 2005

Good Morning. On behalf of the National Board of Directors, I welcome you to our 2005 Installation of Officers ceremony. I am fortunate to work with an outstanding group of dedicated individuals. The Board is comprised of 25 people, who represent numerous chapters from eleven regions across the country, and the National President, Treasurer, and Secretary.

Let me give you a profile of the board members:

2 are former board chairs
4 are retirees
7 are veterans of the military
4 are from the Department of the Army
3 are from the Department of Veterans Affairs
2 are from the Air Force,
And one each from the Department of the Interior, Department of Transportation, Department of Energy, USDA, GSA, City of Seattle, State of Alaska, HUD, FDA, Department of the Navy, Department of Defense, and of course, the Department of State.

Ladies and Gentlemen, the 2005 National Board of Directors:

Mr. Ralph F. Browne, Jr. – Boston, MA
Mr. Daniel Corria – East Providence, RI
Ms. Alma R. Garlington – Ashbury Park, NJ
Ms. Joyce M. Jones – Brooklyn, NY
Ms. Regina D. Kennedy – Baltimore, MD
Ms. Johnita E. Pitts – Belcamp, MD

Ms. C. Jaquie Beatty – Decatur, GA
Dr. Doris P. Sartor, Montgomery, AL
Mr. Oscar L. Williams – Danville, IL
Ms. Ellen G. Dyson – Dayton, OH
Ms. Katherine L. Cage – Houston, TX
Ms. Angela Thorpe-Harris – Duncanville, TX
Ms. Delores Ivy – Florissant, MO
Ms. David C. Hampton – Kansas City, MO
Mr. Gary Blackmon – Denver, CO
Mr. John F. Lyons – Clearfield, UT
Mr. J.B. Larkins – Gardena, CA
Mr. Remond Henderson – Juneau, AK
Mr. Charles Oliver – Federal Way, WA
Mr. J. David Reeves – Fort Washington, MD
Mr. Gerald Reed – Manassas, VA
Ms. Darlene H. Young – Washington, D.C.
Mr. Abe Joseph Jr. – Kingsland, GA
Ms. Cynthia Davis – Pine Bluff, AR

Ladies and Gentlemen – The 2005 National Board of Directors. Thank you.

Appendix G: BIG Reporter – February 2005

ACHIEVING THE FULL GOALS OF BLACKS IN GOVERNMENT

By Farrell J. Chiles
Chair, National Board of Directors

"As long as there is government—there will be—Blacks In Government!"

Thirty years ago, Blacks In Government (BIG) turned the pages of history and began writing a story. A story of challenges and achievements, of commitment and successes, of problems confronted and progress made – a story – without an ending.

Born with a pioneering spirit, an entrepreneurial drive, and a willingness to be bold, BIG's story is one of strength, courage, and triumph. As we celebrate our historic 30th Anniversary, we also welcome in a new dawn – a dawn that symbolizes "an end, as well as a beginning – a renewal as well as a change." This milestone is an inspiration for imminent accomplishments as we focus on excellence in government, community service, professional development, and career progression for all of our members.

While we commemorate the birth of BIG, in February, we also observed Black History Month. This year's theme was *"Celebrating Community: A Tribute to Black Fraternal, Social, and Civic Institutions."* It is appropriate that we celebrate and give tribute to these institutions. Along with our churches and civil rights organizations, they have been the foundation and strength of our black communities. Their history is rich, their achievements are noteworthy, and their leadership in all facets of black life is exemplary.

We are blessed with a wealth of leadership from the black fraternities and sororities, such as J. David Reeves, Vice Chair of the Board of Directors. Phi Beta Sigma; Dawn Lawson, former National Secretary, Alpha Kappa Alpha; Julius Crouch, former National Board Chair, Omega Psi Phi; Dr. Doris Sartor, Executive Vice-President, Delta Sigma Theta; Abe Joseph, former National Treasurer, Alpha Phi Alpha; and Alma Garlington, NTC 2006 Chair, Eta Phi Beta, just to name a few.

BIG members belong to social and civic organizations, such as… LINKS; 100 Black Men; 100 Black Women; Black Surfing Association; National Association for Sickle Cell Disease, Inc.; and Tuskegee Airmen, Inc. At the local levels, our members participate, and provide leadership in a myriad of organizations.

While we celebrate, let us also remember the hundreds of BIG members affected by Hurricanes Katrina and Rita – those who lost loved ones; those who witnessed and experienced the tragedy firsthand; and those who worked tirelessly in the aftermath of the rescue, recovery and assistance efforts. We also thank those who gave financially, delivered services to the evacuees, and helped to restore devastated areas. We're proud of you!

As BIG defends the ideals of equity, excellence, and opportunity, it also continues to shine. In 2005, BIG, not only put on a world-class National Training Conference, but also exhibited financial success, creating a firm foundation for the future! Together, we will continue to move forward and upward, and ultimately achieve the full goals of this esteemed organization.

On behalf of the Board of Directors, I thank you for the trust you have placed in the National Organization of Blacks In Government. And as long as there is government—*there will be*—Blacks In Government!

Appendix H: Delegates Assembly Speech (July 2005)

Greetings Fellow Members:

On behalf of the Board of Directors, I welcome you to the 2005 Blacks In Government National Delegates Assembly (NDA). The NDA is critically important in that it provides a platform for the delegates to promote, advocate, and speak with one voice on behalf of the entire membership. Decisions made here will have broad implications for our organization well into the future.

Blacks In Government, Inc. (BIG) remains a visible, viable, and vocal advocate for the rights and benefits of its members through its efforts in presenting programs, such as the National Training Conference, which address workforce, community, social, and economic issues. These programs educate and thereby assist to eliminate elements of racism and discrimination as well as provide a roadmap to promote equal opportunity.

In 2005, BIG demonstrated, once more, that strategic planning, exemplary professionalism, and quality and effective management are its key tools as it strengthens its position nationwide. We undertook concerted efforts to standardize and improve processes, procedures, and practices that govern the operation of the organization. With respect to expense management, our objectives are simple—monitor expenditures, perform internal audits, and reduce costs. We are equally aggressive in our approach to addressing the needs of our members by actively looking for new projects to achieve new breakthroughs. We are convinced that our focus on innovation, operational excellence, and business execution will prepare us to seize the opportunities that will arise in 2006 and beyond. Our goal is to build an enterprise of which our members can truly be proud. Our challenge is to make sure we stay on top of these developments for the benefit of our members.

My gratitude goes out to those Regional Directors who will step down at the end of the year. We will miss their wise counsel, and we thank them for providing exceptional service during their respective terms of office. You will elect new leaders. It is important that you exercise your responsibility and select individuals who are best qualified to oversee the affairs of your organization.

The Board of Directors welcomes your suggestions, ideas, and comments. We look forward to working with you on the challenges that will emerge in 2006. Together we will continue to move forward and upward, and ultimately achieve the full goals of this esteemed organization.

Thank you for the trust you have placed in the National Organization of Blacks In Government.

Respectfully,

Farrell J. Chiles
Chairman
National Board of Directors

Appendix I: Message from the Chairman of the Board

"As Long as There is Government, There Will be Blacks In Government"

August 20, 2006

Welcome:

On behalf of the Board of Directors, it is with the greatest pleasure and pride that I welcome our fellow Delegates to the 2006 National Delegates Assembly (NDA). The NDA, our highest governing body, is comprised of Delegates who represent a broad range of perspectives, resources, and expertise; who share a compelling vision, and who fulfill an important mission. Our charge is to explore ways in which we can effectively serve the membership, meet our objectives, and exemplify the values and principles we embrace

The NDA plays an integral part in the process of defining and refining Blacks In Government (BIG), and how we may best serve the membership. Our members are very vocal about their opinions and expect their Delegates to be equally vocal on their behalf. Given this responsibility, it is necessary to offer opinions, defend points of view, challenge ideas, take stands on positions, and debate issues in order to arrive at the best solutions. It is entirely appropriate and healthy for us to have differing opinions, and these differences are not only respected, but encouraged.

This year's NDA celebrates a historic milestone—the 30th Anniversary of the incorporation of Blacks In Government (BIG)! For thirty years, BIG has demonstrated the commitment, capacity, and capability to operate at strategic levels, to use our influence effectively, and to lead change. We are committed to upholding this tradition and ensuring a long-lasting legacy that reflects the spirit of BIG.

As my tenure as Board Chair comes to an end this year, I want to offer my thanks to our Board members for their hard work, diligence, and leadership; to our Delegates for their commitment to service and their dedication to representing the interests of our membership; and to the Executive Committee for making my charge easier. It has been a rewarding experience and indeed a pleasure to work with everyone.

For those Board members who are departing, having fulfilled your obligation to BIG—thank you for a job well done. What was accomplished during your term was a necessary process for the advancement of this exceptional organization.

Thank you for taking part in the leadership of this esteemed organization. We look forward to a very productive and exciting Assembly, as we unite in the pursuit of excellence to chart the future course of the National Organization of Blacks In Government.

Sincerely,

Farrell J. Chiles
Chairman, National Board of Directors

Appendix J: Delegates Assembly Speech (August 2006)

Welcome and good afternoon. It is with great pleasure and pride that I speak on behalf of the National Board of Directors and welcome you as we commemorate the 30th anniversary of the incorporation of the National Organization of Blacks In Government.

Thirty years ago BIG turned the pages of history and began writing a story. A story of challenges and achievements, of commitment and successes, of problems confronted and progress made. BIG has served as a catalyst for change in policies that impact human rights, education, and equal opportunity. We have forged powerful partnerships with entities which advance the social, economical, and political status of Black America.

We are proud of all that we have achieved. But today, we have to move forward, take another step, and undertake a new journey to *ensure* a place of influence and pride for BIG—not just across the country, but across the world. The world is not waiting for us–it is evolving and changing. We must be ready to meet new challenges—with new solutions, and new ideas. I am not talking about changes we will need ten years from now. I am talking about today—I'm talking about now.

As we close out this chapter of BIG, we begin another. In this next phase, BIG needs to re-emphasize its commitment to our members, examine current issues of concern to Black America; and assess the impact of national policies on the ability of our members to participate in the national economic life. At the same time, BIG will continue to review its programs and activities to understand where adjustments can be made, and new and valuable initiatives undertaken.

Winston Churchill put it best when he said, "the price of greatness is responsibility." This is where you come in. Our agenda reveals that you not only have a heavy task, but a great responsibility. We have much to discuss about our response to the challenges of a fast-changing world. BIG's role in the world—*and the opportunity to influence its future course*—lies in your hands. Remember, every decision you make at this Assembly, is an investment into our tomorrow. Our success in achieving our mission, vision, and goals will ultimately result from strategies learned from past experiences, creating a roadmap to the future, and ensuring that the interests of our members are never compromised.

I want to give a special welcome to our Delegates who are participating in our Assembly for the very first time. We take encouragement and inspiration from your presence here and do indeed bid you welcome. It's your turn… and the opportunity now exists to use your knowledge, your expertise, your interest, energy, and drive to succeed. We want to hear from you. Your chapter members expect collaboration and expect results.

I doubt if many people would argue about the power of the spoken word; but what about the power of words never spoken? The tongue might be powerful, but so are clenched teeth and a firmly set jaw. Silence can speak volumes we never meant to say. There is a real political reward for bold action—and a serious political cost for standing still. As Frederick Douglass so eloquently stated, "Power concedes nothing without demand. It never did and it never will." I invite you to stay focused, stay informed, and stay engaged. I hope that we fulfill all of your expectations, and I am confident that you will gain great benefits from this experience.

This Assembly is where you take ownership of our organization. As Delegates, you are our policymakers, and will vote on issues that define what BIG is and what it stands for. Rarely will a vote be unanimous, and any differences amongst delegates are not only respected, but encouraged. Conflict is negative only when it is handled poorly. In fact, to a great extent conflict is necessary for progress, and to generate new ideas.

I ask you to join me in fulfilling BIG's destiny. Let us come together – united – in purpose and accomplishment. BIG is our organization. It belongs to us and we belong to it. Let us join together, and make history, once again.

So, as I draw these remarks to a close, let me thank the Delegates of this great organization as well as those who have put their names forward as candidates for the 2006 elections.

As we go into the future, I would be remiss not to thank those leaders who have served us. We are indeed grateful to our Board of Directors. Their professionalism and long-standing commitment to BIG are tributes to the members that they serve.

This year, this body will elect at least 8 new Board members as a result of term limits established by this Assembly in year 2000. It's reassuring to know that some of our Board members will serve as a bridge of continuity that is needed to ensure a smooth transition for your newly elected Board members.

With great pride we want to recognize and show our gratitude to those Board members who will step down this year due to term limits.

From *Region* 1 Mr. Dan Corria; Region 3, Ms. Johnita Pitts; Region 5, Mr. Oscar Williams; Region 6 Ms. Katherine Cage; Region 7, Ms. David Hampton; Region 10 Mr. Charles Oliver; Region 11, Vice Chairman Mr. J. David Reeves; Their wise counsel will be missed. Ladies and gentlemen… Please give them a round of applause.

While we are expressing our appreciation… there has been an enormous amount of work placed into organizing this Assembly; please show your gratitude to Mr. Walton and the NDAT team who has worked day and night to make this Assembly a success.

As my own term limits come to an end this year, I want to thank each of you for the great honor and privilege of serving as your Chairman. I will take with me many memories of a mission that was stimulating, challenging, and rewarding… memories of people who have been confrontational, and sometimes, believe it or not, of those who actually agreed with me.

Let me close with a few personal thoughts. Our history has been one of overcoming challenges, taking advantage of opportunities, and creating new ones where none existed. In losing ourselves in a cause that is greater than ourselves, we join those pathfinders who founded this great organization and our colleagues with whom we labor today, in making a positive difference. I urge all of us to continue to display the *boldness of character* and *strength of spirit* that has defined BIG from its very beginnings. Let's continue our proud history into a future that holds new challenges and *demands* new responses.

For as long as there is inequality… as long as there is injustice… and as long as there is government - there ***will be*** - Blacks In Government.

Thank you for the past, for the present, and may the future be a continuance of that which was established in 1976. It has been my honor and privilege to serve you.

Thank you.

Appendix K: Opening Plenary Speech (NTC 2006)

Good morning distinguished guests; ladies and gentlemen:

It is with great pleasure that I speak on behalf of the Board of Directors and with *equal* pleasure that I stand before you with a great sense of history and humility. This year's conference celebrates an historic milestone—the 30th Anniversary of the *Incorporation* of the *National* Organization of Blacks In Government. From its very beginning—tragedies… challenges… opportunities… *and* triumphs awaited BIG at every turn. But our history has been one of *overcoming* challenges, *taking advantage* of opportunities, and *creating* new ones where none existed.

In honor of our 30th Anniversary of incorporation—and as we document our past, we ask ourselves—what have we accomplished? What has been learned from these three decades of advocacy?

We have learned, beyond a doubt that BIG <u>*is*</u>—a world-class enterprise; that BIG *has* the *commitment*, the *capacity*, and the *capability*--to operate at strategic levels; to promote equal opportunity; to empower and educate people; to further professional growth, to establish global leadership, <u>*and*</u>... to lead change. My friends, because of its passion for excellence—BIG has generated a passion for accomplishment that has even *exceeded* the expectations of its founders!

Reaching up, reaching beyond, and always pressing forward is the passion of the human spirit. In that spirit, we celebrate our successes and give thanks to God for the many people who support our mission of excellence.

We gratefully acknowledge National Training Conference Committee for *organizing* this conference and to all those who have contributed their untiring effort in making our conference a success. Their hard work and commitment to excellence have been essential to the planning, organization, and implementation of this conference.

This year's theme is, "Building <u>*Unity*</u> through Excellence, Growth, and Challenge." One of our greatest strengths is the "unity" of

Blacks In Government. And the best way to building "unity" is to encourage conditions that foster growth, encourage innovation, and help workers invest in new job skills.

There is no better time than now for you to assess your goals, nurture your talents, and pursue advancement within the public and private sectors. Participants have found the NTC experience rewarding—both professionally and politically. Our strategy is to link employers, educational institutions, and workers together in a powerful partnership; identify the emerging growth sectors of our economy, and help workers gain the skills that are in demand by employers *right now*. Educational excellence is ***not*** an option; it is an economic imperative; it is a responsibility; it is a duty.

As you stretch your professional expertise, explore difference contexts and experience, and discover innovative ways of bridging the digital divide in all aspects of BIG's professional priorities, we ask for your feedback. Your comments and insights helped us to refine our programs, to help you reach your goals.

Let us make this conference one of the best in BIG's history and *honor* the ideals on which this organization was founded, keeping in mind our belief in *equality for all* and *privileges for none*.

As we begin another challenging year in the history of BIG, the role that you play, as a member will determine our future. I urge each of you to display the *boldness of character* and *strength of spirit* that has defined BIG from its very beginnings. The *same* unrestrained *courage*, *vision*, and *commitment* it took to get us where we are now—it will take *nothing less* than that—for to *succeed* today.

Let me offer the words of Marian Wright Edelman, in a quote that many ask for:

"The world needs more people who do not have a price at which they can be bought; who do not borrow from integrity to pay for expediency; whose handshake is an ironclad contract; who are not afraid of risks; who are honest in small matters as they are in large ones; whose ambitions are big enough to include others; who know how to win with grace and lose with dignity; who do not believe that shrewdness, cunning, and ruthlessness are the three keys to success; who are not afraid to go against the grain of popular opinion and do not believe in 'consensus'; who are occasionally wrong and always willing to admit it. In short the world needs leaders."

We've only just begun a work that will last a *lifetime*; we ask that you *continue* the battle against inequality for a world of equality; let there be no end to your *courage* or your *commitment,* because as long as there *is* Government—*there will be*—Blacks In Government. I am confident that you are up to the challenge.

Thank you for investing in yourselves, for understanding and embracing the significance of Blacks In Government…and for your uncompromising loyalty to the principles of equity, excellence, and opportunity.

We look forward to a very productive and exciting assembly, as we unite in the pursuit of excellence to chart the future course of Blacks In Government.

Again, welcome, and enjoy your time here. It has always been my honor and privilege to serve you.

Thank you.

INDEX

ABOUT THE AUTHOR

Farrell J. Chiles served as Chairman of the Board of the National Organization of Blacks In Government from 2002-2006. His federal career included positions with the Department of Veterans Affairs and the Department of the Army. In 2007, Farrell was the recipient of the Greater Los Angeles Federal Executive Board's Distinguished Public Service Career Award. He resides in Phillips Ranch, California and can be contacted at farrellchiles@yahoo.com.

Photo Credit for photo appearing above, front cover, and back cover: *Robert Braga/Lasting Images Photography*

CPSIA information can be obtained at www.ICGtesting.com
224015LV00001B/2/P